EMPOWERING TEACHERS WITH TECHNOLOGY

Making It Happen

Michael T. Romano

A SCARECROWEDUCATION BOOK

The Scarecrow Press, Inc.
Lanham, Maryland, and Oxford
2003

A SCARECROWEDUCATION BOOK

Published in the United States of America
by Scarecrow Press, Inc.
A Member of the Rowman & Littlefield Publishing Group
4501 Forbes Boulevard, Suite 200, Lanham, Maryland 20706
www.scarecroweducation.com

PO Box 317
Oxford
OX2 9RU, UK

British Library Cataloguing in Publication Information Available

Library of Congress Cataloging-in-Publication Data

Romano, Michael T. (Michael Thomas), 1924–
    Empowering teachers with technology : making it happen / Michael T.
Romano.
        p. cm.
"A ScarecrowEducation book."
Includes bibliographical references and index.
    ISBN 0-8108-4629-2 (pbk. : alk. paper)
    1. Educational technology—United States. 2. Teachers—Effect of
technological innovations on—United States. I. Title.
LB1028.3 .R646 2003
371.33—dc21   2002015494

$\otimes^{TM}$ The paper used in this publication meets the minimum requirements of
American National Standard for Information Sciences—Permanence of Paper
for Printed Library Materials, ANSI/NISO Z39.48-1992.
Manufactured in the United States of America.

"This book is written in a style that should appeal to a broad audience: teachers, administrators, people in the government, concerned parents, and others who have a vested interest in how our youth learn. Dr. Romano's insights go beyond the classroom and reflect a broad range of meaningful experiences in a career of more than forty years."—Raymond C. Bard, dean emeritus and founder, school of allied health sciences, Medical College of Georgia

"The most profound message of this book is the admonition that failure to acknowledge the seminal role of the teacher, regardless of the technology in vogue, is to consign education to a future of continuing unmet expectations."—Alvin L. Morris, dean emeritus and founder, college of dentistry, University of Kentucky

"As you read and understand the promise of Dr. Romano's work, it will become obvious that what he has projected is more than just another approach; it is an ingenious, comprehensive program for dealing with the formidable challenge of effectively utilizing technology in our schools."—Michael H. Pelosi, chief executive officer and founder (ret.), Airo Clean Engineering, Inc., Exton, Pennsylvania

"The simplicity of Dr. Romano's Technology-Enhanced Curriculum guarantees the effective and successful transformation of our nineteenth century classroom into a twenty-first century environment with a multi-sensory learning opportunity for every student. Creative-thinking leaders, parents, and teachers will find this book fascinating and extremely meaningful."—Marti L. Wilson, middle school teacher, Williamsburg, Kentucky Independent School District

To my parents, Nicandro and
Rosina. As a child, nothing but
my best would satisfy them.
Now I am grateful.

CONTENTS

FOREWORD

I first met Dr. Michael T. Romano while I was president of the Kentucky Education Association. He visited my office in Frankfort, Kentucky, and our discussion was a lively camaraderie of the potential and the power of truly incorporating technology into the classroom curriculum. He shared his vision with me and talked of his research and goals. I was impressed, but more importantly, I became renewed and excited as I listened to a professor emeritus at the University of Kentucky, my first alma mater.

Dr. Romano described a practical, effective, commonsense approach to how teachers should integrate technology into their teaching. He didn't talk about the usual culprits—hardware, training, and funding. We talked about excitement and productivity, a characteristic and a result of successful teaching and learning. Dr. Romano explained to me that the academic model he calls the *Technology-Enhanced Curriculum* is built on the cornerstone of developing software that would be "curriculum-integrated, custom-designed, and course-specific." His enthusiasm was contagious and his goals of completing his book, *Empowering Teachers with Technology,* and providing leadership for implementing a classroom demonstration of his concept were well defined. The book is one that every teacher should read, and I am certain the software he will be developing should be considered a collection of excellence under construction.

Our meeting that day set my mental energy into a spin of thoughts. I agreed with the vision Dr. Romano shared on that spring morning. I applaud his efforts to tackle more challenges in his illustrious career, and I appreciate his concern for empowering teachers instead of—as some do—blaming them for many of the limitations of our educational system.

I have the highest regard for teachers, perhaps because they were my colleagues for 25 years and we shared something very special. Teachers want their students to experience success in the classroom; we are nurtured by their personal successes. Failure is not our goal. However, we find ourselves locked in the intense frustration of failed attempts to understand the power and excitement of technology and the Internet and how these resources can be integrated into the curriculum.

Our students spend their out-of-class life immersed in technology. Their computer skills often far exceed those of their teachers. It is irrational to believe that we teachers can continue the teaching practices of the last century and prepare our students for the demands and jobs of the Digital Age. Our students will fail to learn the content and application if we teachers fail to appropriately incorporate technology into our lessons.

We have yet to pull all the pieces together so we can meet *our own* expectations and those global expectations placed upon public education. The federal government and individual states have spent billions of dollars on our efforts to integrate technology, but undoubtedly we have fallen short. We still suffer the agony of isolated knowledge and skills and the frustration of not knowing what will work. Shying away from the techno-geeks has been our unfounded response to the fear that the mighty microchip will somehow replace classroom teachers.

Dr. Michael Romano has spent years with the techno-geeks and has himself become one in his determination to understand why technology is not being successfully integrated into the curriculum. He has analyzed the failures of the last 50 years and has fostered solutions engineered for practitioners—classroom teachers. His finely honed insights help us to focus and define a coherent vision of how technology should be used by teachers, and his approach will undoubtedly bring a surge of excitement to the classroom.

Romano's book, *Empowering Teachers with Technology,* is both a vision and a method. It is an answer to the chaotic and often ineffective state of technology integration in the classroom. It is so simple, yet profound, that one must ask why we haven't already produced course-specific software for every class or at least for every class that addresses core curricula. In the use of course-specific software, teachers are involved in the production of the software and serve as the resource specialists. Teachers in the classroom utilize the software, incorporate it in computer labs, and, at all times, retain their traditional control of the class. This interfacing of technology, classroom teacher, technologist, and students provides for individualized monitoring and mentoring; provides immediate feedback; provides for increased student expectations; and inevitably provides for increased student achievement, the bottom line.

Expectedly, the *Technology-Enhanced Curriculum* requires a new and costly teacher-support system. The model already exists. Empowering physicians, pilots, bankers, and other professionals with technology required the creation of complex, costly support systems. We must do the same for teachers. Our youth deserve no less.

I believe that Dr. Romano is on the right track. I think he has configured a solution—the academic model—that has escaped us for too long. Working with a consortium of educators from Williamsburg, Kentucky; Kentucky Educational Television; the University of Kentucky College of Education; and Academic Software, Inc., Dr. Romano is mounting a classroom demonstration of his new model. He has captured the essence of his research and vision in his latest publication, *Empowering Teachers with Technology*. In his concept, the teacher's role is amplified, not diminished, and the fear of technology is removed because no major retraining of teachers is necessary. Teachers can access the Technology-Enhanced Curriculum software and become conductors for textbooks, lectures, discussions, the Internet, and all other media. Romano's model utilizes television in an interactive format called Teacher-Narrated Video. With what he describes as Computerized Remedial Tutoring, teachers can provide as much individualized instruction and additional assistance as a particular learner needs. Makeup work becomes a fresh, vital endeavor.

Being a teacher is not an easy job. Rather, it is a most demanding calling, and we, the stakeholders, must provide our teachers with the best resources so they can teach our most precious possession—our children and grandchildren. Providing our teachers with curriculum-specific software is the essential missing tool. We simply must create the system to develop it and put it into the hands of those with whom we entrust the future.

Judith Rose Gambill
Past President, Kentucky Education Association

PREFACE

The year was 1956 and as a young dental educator, I faced the challenge of teaching a class of 140 learners how to operate on an individual tooth situated within the confines of the oral cavity. I did what my teachers had done for me and their teachers had done for them: I circled 10 or 12 learners around a dental chair and proceeded to demonstrate my clinical skills. How much did they see? Obviously, it was not very much. And I faced the chore of repeating the procedure a dozen times or so.

Then I was empowered by the technological marvel of that day—closed-circuit television. Now, 140 learners sat in a lecture/demonstration theater as I escorted them into the mouth and virtually into the decay to be removed from the tooth. I have been a true educational "techno-geek" for almost half a century.

A footnote: incredibly, today there are still dental students who huddle around a dental chair, straining for a peek at what their teacher is doing inside a cavity, in a tooth inside a mouth. Without a doubt, in education allegiance to tradition endures—and endures.

This book represents a six-year effort coming at the conclusion of a 40-year career in education. The research for this work started in 1994 and includes 52 articles and 67 books published over a span of years from 1956 to 2002. Thus, it reflects the collective wisdom and experience of countless individuals.

In reality, preparation for this work began in 1961. Then, I was commissioned by the U.S. Office of Education to study the use of closed-circuit television in the medical and dental schools of America. Over a period of two years, I visited 23 academic health centers. That project initiated my long-term preoccupation with the potential of technology to empower teachers at all levels and enhance learner achievement.

The extensive literature search initiated in 1994 was augmented by the on-site study of 17 schools ranging from primary to graduate education. Countless teachers, administrators, and learners have shared their views and contributed to *my perception* of present-day realities.

This book suggests where we need to go with educational technology based on a review—a 50-year review of where we have been.

ACKNOWLEDGMENTS

I didn't realize until I started this book in 1994 that, in fact, over the years there had evolved an impressive network of fine minds as part of my life. And, when I needed them, they were there for me.

Barry D. Kaufman, D.M.D., is a doctor of dental medicine who became one of the nation's eminent health reporters. His award-winning coverage on television and radio spans all aspects of health care. Early on, he urged me to put aside my "professional literature style" and write with the deep feeling he knew I harbored for this particular subject. Barry has been in my life since 1969.

Five people contributed their time and talent as a panel of experts. As we discussed each draft and each conclusion, I asked that they be liberal with the red pencil—and they were.

Raymond C. Bard, Ph.D., is a microbiologist who spent the first part of his 40-year career in the pharmaceutical industry before being enticed into higher education. He has served in a number of high-level posts in academics and recently retired as dean emeritus and founder, School of Allied Health Sciences, Medical College of Georgia. We have shared our lives since 1952 when he came to my dental practice with a mouth full of needy teeth and gums.

Alvin L. Morris, D.D.S., Ph.D., has earned national recognition as an academician, a researcher, an administrator, and an oral health care

delivery specialist. His first major appointment was to serve as found-
ing dean of the University of Kentucky College of Dentistry in 1961.
He then moved on to a number of leadership positions in higher education and professional organizations. I am one of the many whose career has been enriched by this individual. Al has been part of my life
since 1956.

Michael H. Pelosi Jr., B.S., P.E., is an engineer who founded and
headed a prominent manufacturing company in the Clean Room industry. He holds 10 major patents in his technological specialty. Currently,
he serves on the steering committee of a local group known as Taxpay-
ers for Educational Accountability. Michael and I were boys together
and have been in close touch since 1936.

Ronald E. Walton, Ed.D., is a schoolteacher who became superintendent of the school system in Lexington, Kentucky. Now, he is retired,
and I was fortunate to have him on my team. He has been my "reality
check." His wisdom and experience have been invaluable in steering me
through several difficult junctures.

The final collaborator is Marti L. Wilson, B.S., M.A. She is our real-
life educator who toils daily "in the vineyard." As a middle-school
teacher, her insights have been extremely meaningful. Marti is the wife
of my pastor and special friend, Reverend Ward Wilson. Ward has also
taken an interest in my work and has been generous along the way in offering encouragement and spiritual support.

My grandson Brian Teague has contributed as my computer guru.
Early on, when my mind had become clogged with all that I had read,
he helped me sort it all out and has been there for me ever since. Brian
has admitted for several years that he is a genuine techno-geek. I keep
telling him he is more—much more—than that label implies.

Mary Ellen Gardner is the talented person who painstakingly fin-
gered pages and pages of my scribbling into that incredible computer of
hers. This great lady dedicated six years of conscientious effort to this
work, and I am truly grateful.

Daniel P. Calvisi of New York is a writer and literary consultant. He
reviewed the first draft and rendered a page-by-page critique. I have
come to value his insights a great deal.

Ann Stockham retired from the editorial staff of a major medical journal. In 1999, I met her as a new neighbor and convinced her to pick up

her red pencil again and lend her keen mind and fine hand to these pages. This was, indeed, a stroke of good fortune for me.

Yvette Dale Pickett was by my side for two revisions. In addition to her skills at the keyboard, this conscientious and enthusiastic young woman came forth with a number of meaningful suggestions that added to the value of this work.

My wife, Anne, has graciously tolerated living under the same roof with my mistress—the book. It has been my primary preoccupation for several years and, at the least, it has tested the strength of our marriage.

Finally, to my many teachers, from Miss Mary Gallagher in first grade, to Dr. Raymond G. Walter, my dental school adviser: this work is the fruit of the seeds you sowed so many years ago. From my heart— thank you.

1

A TIME FOR NEW STRATEGIES

We were the first nation to pursue the dream of education for all;
and it has made a difference.

—Michael T. Romano

AN OPENING PERSPECTIVE

Our educational system has served us well. It produced those who
landed on the moon, those who routinely replace diseased hearts with
healthy ones, and, in reality, it has cultivated the minds of all who have
created the many marvels of twenty-first-century civilization.

When viewed in the broadest context, the United States has emerged
as the world's only superpower, and it can be speculated that its eminence is primarily attributable to three factors: the richness of its human
and natural resources, its passion for individual freedom and equality,
and, above all, its educational system. We were the first nation to pursue the dream of education for all, and it has made a difference.

Thus, it should be acknowledged at the outset: the educational system
in place works. How well does it work? Perhaps it works as well as the

air-travel system worked before propellers were replaced by jet power. And the challenge is to do for teaching and learning what has been done for air travel: find the way to propel it to a new evolutionary level. A way to help teachers transform the books, chalkboard, teacher-talk classroom model developed in the Industrial Age to a model in context with the Digital Age. Undoubtedly, for 50 years we have tried; again and again.

And yet, all of our effort, determination, and riches are not enough to do for teachers what has been done for physicians, pilots, bankers, and other professionals: amplify their capacity to function by *empowering them with technology.*

TEACHERS AND TECHNOLOGY

At the beginning of the twenty-first century, how we live, work, and recreate are being transformed by a powerful, pervasive, global force—technology. Teaching and learning is an information-driven process. The teacher's prime responsibility is to manage the information required to meet the objectives of a specific curriculum. Digital Age technology facilitates the storage, transmission, and retrieval of information in multimedia and on an individualized, interactive basis.

It is logical to assume it should have a central role in what teachers do. Still, the facts are incontrovertible. After 50 years of costly trial and error, technology is still not an integral, routine part of what happens in the classroom. Stated another way: we have not yet found the way to connect education and technology so that teachers might do what they do more effectively.

To keep this matter in perspective, it should be noted that billions have been spent for technology in schools. In 1999, the CEO Forum, a school-reform advocacy group financed by 20 of the nation's leading corporations, published its *School Technology and Readiness Report.* It concludes: "The gap between technology presence in schools and its effective use is still too wide. We continue to believe the quality of public education depends upon our collective ability to close the gap between technology presence and its effective use in the pursuit of school improvement."[1]

Based on a 50-year analysis, this book addresses why the gap exists and what needs to be done to close it.

THE INCONTROVERTIBLE FACTS

Major spending for educational technology began in the 1950s. Here are some facts:

- In 1952, the National Defense Education Act provided $27 million (equivalent to $4 billion in 2002) to connect every classroom in the United States to a system of state educational television networks.
- From 1998 to 2002, the federal government spent $7.95 billion to connect classrooms to the Internet.
- From 1958 to 1995, the federal government spent $14.1 billion for programs intended to promote the use of educational technology.
- In FY2001, the U.S. Department of Education budgeted $872 million for technology in the classroom.
- In FY2000, the state expenditures for educational technology in the United States totaled $5.7 billion.
- From 1991 to 2000, the relatively small Commonwealth of Kentucky spent $660 million to support the use of technology in the classroom.

Not included is the money spent by philanthropic foundations and major corporations. Undoubtedly, the billions invested in the past 50 years underscore the view that technology does have a vital role in enhancing learner achievement. Where are we in defining that role? Here are the facts from authoritative sources:

- 1995, the U.S. Congress Office of Technology Assessment. After decades of costly trial and error, teachers and administrators still need a vision of how technology can best be deployed.[2]
- 1996, the Apple Classroom of Tomorrow project. In the maze of reform efforts, the role of technology remains unclear.[3]
- 1999, the Milken Exchange on Education Technology Study. Digital resources are bursting on the scene, but no one is quite sure how to effectively use them.[4]

- 2002, the U.S. Department of Education announces it will conduct a three-year, $15 million study to determine "how best to integrate technology into the classroom."[5]

The facts are, indeed, incontrovertible. For 50 years, billions have been spent to boost learner achievement by empowering teachers with technology. However, there has not as yet emerged a clear vision regarding how to effectively integrate the costly hardware and software into what routinely happens in the classroom. The frustration level in the educational establishment and beyond has become increasingly palpable.

THE NEED FOR A SHARED VISION

Edward Cornish, president of the World Future Society, writing about education in 1980, noted—perhaps somewhat idealistically—that we need a great dream: "A *vision* of a future that will be so compellingly desirable that we will all feel responsible for its realization. And we will go forward confidently." He concluded, "I feel positive that we can create such a vision, and that is why I remain optimistic about the future. The future is dark only because we have not yet created light, but we can create light and I believe that we will."[6]

That was 1980, and there is still no discernible vision. In 1996, Steven W. Gilbert, director of technology at the American Association for Higher Education, made a plea to harness the insights of all those who understand current patterns of change in teaching, learning, and technology to help shape "a *vision* worth working toward."[7]

THE SEARCH

Following a 40-year career as an academician that included hands-on experience in adapting technology to the classroom and the teaching laboratory, I set out to seek answers to these straightforward, yet vexing questions:

- Specifically, how does technology empower teachers and thereby improve learner achievement?

- Why has the 50-year effort to integrate technology into the classroom along with "books, chalkboard, and teacher-talk" failed to meet expectations?
- Based on this analysis, can an approach to effectively connect teachers, learners, and technology be devised?
- What implementation strategy is required to help teachers transform the Industrial Age model of education to a new Digital Age model?

These questions represent an old challenge. Finding the answers required a six-year effort that included:

- An extensive review of the literature. This consisted of 67 books and 52 articles published from 1956 to 2002. It reflects the collective wisdom and experience of some of the world's leading authorities on education and the system that supports it.
- An on-site study of 17 schools, ranging from primary to graduate education. Teachers, administrators, and learners shared their views and contributed to my perception of present-day realities.
- The collaboration of a five-person panel of experts representing a wide range of experiences. Two were retired college deans; one had been the superintendent of a public school system; another was a retired corporate CEO active in local school district affairs; and the last was a working middle-school teacher. They participated in numerous consultations, reviewed each chapter of the book as it was written, and provided critical feedback.
- Discussions with three major "players" on the national education scene: the director of the Technology Center at the National Education Association; the assistant to the director of educational technology at the U.S. Department of Education; and a vice president at IBM who directs its multimillion-dollar Reinventing Education Program. These individuals provided a valuable perspective in that they represent three powerful, legitimate, vested interests, each with its own agenda.

The research for this book provides subjective findings and perceptions derived from what has been observed firsthand and the opinions of others as reported in the literature and related directly. Admittedly, all of this has been influenced by the insights and perceptions my colleagues and I have reaped from decades of experience in almost all aspects of the teaching-learning enterprise. Most important, this work proposes new strategies based on an analysis of the past half century, from educational television to computers and the Internet.

LEARNING FROM THE ACOT STUDY

In 1986, the landmark Apple Classroom of Tomorrow (ACOT) project was launched with great fanfare and expectations. It involved some of the nation's leading education theorists, backed by the resources of a major, global corporation—Apple Computer.

The objective was to determine, conclusively, the most effective use of technology in the classroom. Ten years and undisclosed millions of dollars later, one of the several books documenting this unprecedented experience referred to "stages of instructional evolution."[8] Based on their research, two stages can be defined:

- Stage 1—*Adaptation:* Technology is thoroughly integrated into the classroom in support of existing practice.
- Stage 2—*Transformation:* Technology is a catalyst for significant changes in learning practice; students and teachers adopt new roles and relationships.

The ACOT study was one of the most important of its kind in recent years. By its own admission, it "failed to meet expectations." Subsequently, it will be reviewed in depth. At this point, however, it should be noted that although it suggested a broadly defined two-stage strategy for phasing technology into schools, it stopped short of actually bringing forth a new working model of education.

BEYOND THE ACOT STUDY

Based on the platform suggested by the ACOT project, our work addresses the adaptation and transformation stages of instructional evolution, proposing a model for each.

- The *Technology-Enhanced Curriculum.* This model provides teachers a template for adapting—or retrofitting—existing curricula to technology currently found in schools. It is an entry-level approach developed by analyzing what technology does and what teachers traditionally do, and then carefully integrating them. Basically, it is an interim model that puts in place enabling measures required for the final-stage transformation model.
- The *Technology-Dependent Curriculum.* It is the ultimate Digital Age model of education. It deploys the full power of technology to restructure, or to transform, the model in place. As the term implies, it is not operational without the use of technology. Most important, the teacher emerges with a markedly amplified capacity to function. It should be noted that it represents an increment of change far beyond what the existing system could tolerate in one "leap." Thus, the need to put in place the interim, or adaptation, model.

The history of change in education indicates it is unrealistic to expect that the final stage described here can be put in place in less than a decade after the course has been set. Hopefully, this book takes the first step. It defines the goal and suggests an implementation strategy.

ONE FINAL THOUGHT

The 1996 report of the Apple Classroom of Tomorrow experience states, "No one has the incentive to look back, to study failures, to salvage what worked, to fix what didn't and avoid making the same mistake next time."[9]

The research for this book looks back more than 50 years, and what emerges is the *vision* of an evolutionary Digital Age model of education.

NOTES

1. CEO Forum, *School Technology and Readiness Report.* Washington, DC: CEO Forum, February 1999.

2. U.S. Congress, Office of Technology Assessment, *Teachers and Technology: Making the Connection.* OTA-HER-616, Washington, DC: U.S. Government Printing Office, 1995, p. 125.

3. Fisher, C., Dwyer, D., and Yocam, K., *Education and Technology.* San Francisco: Apple Press, 1996, p. 97.

4. Fatemi, E., ed., "Building the Digital Curriculum," in *Technology County* '99, supplement to *Education Week.* September 23, 1999, p. 6.

5. Trotter, Andrew, "Department Study to Examine Effectiveness of Technology," *Education Week,* February 6, 2002, p. 23.

6. Cornish, Edward, "Foreword," in *Education: A Time for Decisions,* ed. Kathleen M. Redd and Arthur M. Harkins. Washington, DC: World Future Society, 1980, p. v.

7. Gilbert, Steven W., "Making the Most of a Slow Revolution," *Change.* March/April 1996, p. 23.

8. Sandholtz, J., Ringstaff, C., and Dwyer, D., *Teaching with Technology.* New York: Teachers College Press, 1997, p. 37.

9. Fisher, Dwyer, and Yocam, *Education and Technology,* p. 97.

WORLDS APART: THE TECHNOLOGY GAP IN THE CLASSROOM

Human beings have always been conditioned to learn under the guidance of other humans.

—Michael T. Romano

About this chapter:

- It notes that there is a technology gap between the classroom and the world beyond its walls.
- It underscores the extent of the gap by reviewing the expectations regarding education and technology.
- It provides views that confirm the reality that technology has not yet become an essential, integral part of the classroom.
- It emphasizes the importance of maintaining uncompromised the traditional teacher–learner bond.
- It discusses the technology gap as a serious impediment to learners, which has not been generally acknowledged.
- It defines a "technohumanistic" system and notes the similarity between its application in education and in health care.
- It offers the view that there should be no revolutions in education but, rather, managed evolution.

TWO WORLDS

Outside the classroom, young people today exist in an electronic symbiotic relationship with a wide array of on-demand, mind-grabbing marvels. Their technology-rich world includes multisource video; computer-generated, interactive imagery of all descriptions; and the compelling reality of cyberspace. This is the awesome Digital Age, and the young become technically versatile with ease and enthusiasm. Actually, it is as though some develop a virtual dependency on their linkage to a seductive, electronic universe brought to their eyes and ears by television, computers, and the Internet. The elite of this generation like to be referred to as "techno-geeks."

Then, there is the world of the classroom. There, for the most part, the routine centers on books, chalkboards, and teacher-talk. It was so for our parents, our grandparents, and their parents. In today's Digital Age, this is perplexing.

Yet, for most of the twentieth century there have been loud voices that insist teachers, learners, and technology would form an enduring, meaningful union. As the twenty-first century begins, there is ample evidence this has not happened—the old order has survived.

THE UNREALIZED EXPECTATIONS

Cohen says it best: "New technology is an old educational enchantment."[1] How old? The year was 1913 when expectations were raised by the "Wizard of Menlo Park" himself—Thomas Edison. How far out on a limb did he venture? Very, very far.

"I believe the motion picture is destined to revolutionize our educational system," he proclaimed confidently. Then, he ventured still further, "Books will soon be obsolete in schools. Scholars will be instructed through the eye. It is possible to teach every branch of human knowledge with the motion picture."[2]

Considering the source, this attracted wide attention and raised high expectations. And that was in 1913. Throughout most of the twentieth century, each time a new advance in information technology made the scene, it happened: revolutions were heralded and expectations were raised—only to be dashed again and again.

- 1932: Radio is "the assistant teacher." We now have "Textbooks of the Air." The roof of the classroom has been blown off and its walls have been set on the circumference of the globe.[3]
- 1950: When the eye and the ear have been remarried by television, then we shall indeed be challenged to open wide the school door. There will be no "blindness gap" to be bridged.[4]
- 1960: Teaching machines (programmed instruction) will revolutionize the schools. The process of education will be improved immeasurably.[5]
- 1969: As surely as books changed education, television and technology will revolutionize it. The signs are everywhere, including the pressure on education by students, parents, and teachers to change.[6]
- 1980: If the schools fail to embrace the new technologies of computers and other technological communications systems—that technology will put them out of business. Time after time in our society, new technologies have wiped out old industries.[7]
- 1986: The age of schooling is over. A new postindustrial technological "learning enterprise" is about to replace the outworn infrastructure. What we now call "school" will have as much place in the twenty-first century's learning system as the horse and buggy have in today's transportation system.[8]
- 1994: Fortunately, the information technology revolution is creating a new form of electronic multimedia: interactive education that should blossom into a lifelong learning system that allows almost anyone to learn almost anything, from anywhere, at any time. The type of schools that educated youngsters in the past will soon be gone forever.[9]

Obviously, Edison and the other pundits were wrong. The revolutions never happened. Empowering teachers with technology remains an elusive goal. The old order endures.

THE "FOURTH REVOLUTION" IS DECLARED

It was back in 1972 when the Carnegie Commission on Higher Education rendered a landmark judgment on the potential of technology in education. It included individuals highly qualified to make judgments on matters related to education: six university presidents, three professors of education, two chief executive officers of major corporations, three heads of education-affiliated foundations, a former state governor, a professor of psychology, and the master of a college in Cambridge, England.

The commission's widely read report was entitled *The Fourth Revolution: Instructional Technology in Higher Education.*[10] The title was based on the four revolutions in education defined in 1967 by Sir Eric Ashby, the master of Clare College, Cambridge, England:

- The first revolution occurred when the task of educating the young was shifted, in part, from parents to teachers and from the home to the school.
- The second was when the use of the written word was permitted to coexist with the spoken word in the classroom. Teachers who did not have the capacity to write resisted the writings of others.
- The third revolution came from the invention of printing and the subsequent wide availability of books.
- The fourth revolution is portended by the incredible breakthroughs in information technology.

The Carnegie Commission's report offered an unprecedented, unqualified endorsement of the potential of technology: "We are confident that expanding the use of instructional technology will improve learning, make teaching and learning more challenging to students and teachers alike, and yield cost savings as it becomes widely deployed and reduces the need for live instruction."[11]

That was 1972, and again enormous expectations were raised. Understandably, it also raised anxiety among those who earn their livelihood in the classroom—teachers.

THE REVOLUTION IN RETROSPECT

Today, the Fourth Revolution still waits in the wings. But much has been done in the attempt to bring technology center stage. Primarily, billions of dollars for research, teacher training, hardware, and software have been poured into education at all levels. And then, in 1995, the Office of Technology Assessment of the U.S. Congress issued a widely circulated report on the use of technology in the nation's schools. It offered this conclusion:

> Despite decades of investment in educational hardware and software, relatively few of the nation's 2.8 million teachers use technology in their teaching. Helping schools make the connection between teachers and technology may be the most important step in making the most of past, present and future investments in education and in our children's future.[12]

This statement implies that, in fact, there exists an understanding of how to "make the connection." In reality, our work concludes this is not the case, in spite of the decades of costly research and demonstration projects.

The experience of the Apple Classroom of Tomorrow (ACOT) project validated this conclusion. As noted earlier, this project was the most extensive effort of its kind since the educational television experiments of the 1960s. The preface of the 10-year report published in 1996 candidly states: "There is much ambiguity whether technology's role in education will continue to increase. In the maze of education reform, the role of technology in education remains *unclear*."[13]

However, one thing is clear: teaching and learning is an information-driven process, in an age when advances in information technology are literally mind-boggling. There must be a vital connection between teachers, learners, and technology. Determining how to empower teachers with technology is the key to achieving broad-based, quantifiable improvement in how our youth learn.

Another thing is certain: there has been no breakthrough, and the gap between the classroom and the technology-dependent world it serves is widening at an increasingly rapid rate. This is as difficult to rationalize and potentially as hazardous as traveling today's superhighways in a horse and buggy. In 1994, Thornburg warned: "The grace period is over. No longer can we allow outdated institutions to proceed at a snail's pace into a future zooming ahead at the speed of light. The gap is already stretched to the limit, and the thread connecting many current schools to society's needs is about to break."[14]

THE CRITICAL RIGHT/LEFT BRAIN MATTER

In the book *Beyond the Classroom: Why School Reform Has Failed,* a group of social scientists reports that there are objective data from national surveys that indicate teachers are facing a growing number of students who come to school less interested, less motivated, and less engaged in the business of learning.[15]

This observation, in itself, is not remarkable. However, coupled to a growing body of knowledge regarding the roles of the right and left brain hemispheres, it leads to a conclusion that might be at the root of why some of our youth have difficulty learning in the classroom. For decades, it has been clearly established that humans have two separate, linked information-processing systems. The left brain deals exclusively with sounds and digits—words; the right brain, with pictures and graphics—images.

The relationship between this phenomenon and learning has been noted since 1972.[16] In 1983, Williams made this observation: "In their early years, children use all their senses to learn about the world. They handle a new object, look at it from all sides, listen to any sounds it makes, smell it and often put it in their mouths both to taste it and explore it with their tongues. They take in information through all their senses."[17]

However, in the classroom, where for the most part it is books, chalkboard, and teacher-talk, the great preponderance of the sensory inputs is to the left brain—the half that deals primarily with words. Thus, it appears our educational system, and our understanding of intelligence, discriminates against one half of the brain and, consequently, tends to reward only left brain-dominant learners who respond well to verbal, linear styles of teaching.

In 1998, Freed and Parsons in their book *Right-Brained Children in a Left-Brained World* sharpened the focus on this critical matter. Some key points:

- Why are we facing a crisis in education? Students today are fundamentally different: our classrooms are being flooded by a new generation of right-brained, visual kids. While our school system plods along using the same teaching methods that were in vogue decades ago, students are finding it more and more difficult to learn that way. As our culture becomes more visual and our brain dominance shifts to the right, the chasm widens between teacher and pupil. Our schools are no longer congruent with the way many children think.

- The twenty-first-century child is the product of a culture that bombards us with rapid-fire images. From birth, his environment literally wires and rewires visual pathways to the brain.
- Some educators point to the 1960s as the time when our schools "collapsed." That time coincides with the first generation of children raised with television.
- If we have any hope of reaching the growing population of right-brained children, we have to understand how they think and learn.[18]

This is indeed leading-edge thinking. There is little indication the education establishment has yet grasped the enormous significance of the right/left brain matter. In great part, it justifies the use of technology in education. Simply, in addition to much more, it allows teachers to routinely create visually rich experiences for learners.

The matter of words versus pictures in the classroom is discussed further subsequently. Additionally, a whole-brain, Digital Age model of education and a two-phased implementation strategy is proposed.

Finally, a question: who would choose to sit in the living room listening to the news on radio rather than listening to and looking at television? Yet, in schools everywhere, everyday, children are made to spend hours listening to a teacher standing at a chalkboard, valiantly attempting to make vivid the universe of yesterday, today, and tomorrow. That same teacher, empowered with technology, can make what happens in the classroom as compelling as what happens in the world beyond its walls.

THE TRADITIONAL TEACHER–LEARNER BOND

Strategies for change in what happens in the classroom must be based on the truth that human beings have always been conditioned to learn under the guidance of other humans.

From the moment we open our eyes as "babes in arms," our dependency begins. Hand in hand with others, we learn to walk, to talk, and to acquire basic self-sufficiency. Teaching and learning appear to be driven by emulation, shared aspirations, and the human need to impact the well-being of others. Thus, the relationship between teacher and learner has the potential to become intimate and nurturing; a special bond between someone with a "felt" need to learn and grow and someone dedicated to help meet that need. There seems little doubt that, to some extent, this conditioning endures throughout our lives.

Some believe technology may compromise the traditional teacher–learner bond. It should be noted, however, that the most user-friendly and effective technological systems are those that skillfully blend technical and human elements. For example, a heart could not be transplanted without augmenting the surgeon's knowledge and skill with a host of highly sophisticated technological systems supported by teams of auxiliaries. Yet, before an operation, the surgeon's visit to the bedside to reassure the anxious patient has become an essential part of the total procedure. Thus, health care today can best be described as a true tech-nohumanistic system.

The model of education to be introduced maintains the teacher's traditional, fundamental role—uncompromised. Like surgeons and airline pilots, teachers will continue to function as the central figures in the system. Like their counterparts, however, their capacity to function will be markedly amplified by technology. And, above all, it will be shown that this can evolve in a manner that preserves what is best in our system of education: *the magical and essential interface between teacher and learner.*

GOBEL, THE INTERSTATES, REVOLUTIONS, AND COMPATIBILITY

What is the elusive key to connecting teachers, learners, and technology? In the middle 1960s, Saturday night television belonged to "Lonesome George" Gobel. This droll midwesterner was clever, sly, and often very perceptive of the human condition. His most memorable admonishment was "You can't get there from here!" Everyone laughed at him.

Now, it has come to pass that some in the education establishment should have taken Gobel seriously.

Over the past several decades there have been various attempts to describe, and in a number of instances implement, new, revolutionary educational systems. Perelman, among others, proposes what he refers to as a technology-driven "hyperlearning system." He contends that it should replace what he portrays as an obsolete system of teachers, administrators, and facilities.[19] Although his concept may have merit, it has one significant flaw. As Lonesome George said simply, "You can't get there from here!"

The corporate giant IBM has put in place a long-term, multimillion-dollar program it calls Reinventing Education. The objective is to replace the existing system with a new technology-intensive model. Although its motive is commendable, it too seems to have failed to heed Gobel's admonishment. There is no way the educational system in place can be demolished and carted away like an old building. Without a doubt, the new must be linked firmly to what exists, or there can be no change.

An analogy is the development of the interstate highway system in the United States. In the 1950s, a functional highway system—albeit outmoded—was in place and obviously had to remain in place. This represented a tangible barrier, or limitation, to the degree of feasible change. Thus, the new roads had to be literally interwoven with the old.

And so it is with education. There can be no revolution in education, only skillfully managed evolution. This has been referred to in the literature as the "compatibility factor."[20] The research for this book and my years as an educator have led to this seminal conclusion: The routine, broad-scaled use of technology in education can only be achieved by a strategy based on a realistic appraisal of the existing system's capacity to assimilate change, not the perceived capacity of technology to create new and superior systems. Further, it must be underscored that teachers are the critical factor in achieving change. If it is to be widely adopted, innovation must be carefully folded into what teachers have been trained to do, what they can be easily retrained to do, what they believe is best for their learners, and what they believe is best for their careers, as well as the requirements of the curriculum in place and the constraints of the classroom support system. This is the *compatibility factor*.

After studying decades of failure to achieve broad-scaled, quantifiable education reform, Reiser offered this opinion:

> Our public education system has built up complex mechanisms that serve to maintain and support it. They exist in the form of administrative structures, organizational and cultural norms, and even legislative policies. That is why innovations are either adapted to fit the existing system, or else they are sloughed off, allowing the system to remain essentially untouched.[21]

Finally, in 1972, John Gardner, a former secretary of the U.S. Department of Health, Education, and Welfare and a widely respected education guru of that day, made a statement that reverberated in the lay and professional literature for many years: "The pieces for a true revolution in education are strewn about us everywhere—waiting to be assembled."[22] At that time I had been an academic techno-geek for more than 15 years. Like many, I found his utterance to be profound and provocative. Now, more than a quarter of a century later, it is obvious there has been no revolution, no "great leap" in education.

Webster's dictionary defines *revolution* simply as "a sudden, radical, or complete change." After 40 years as an educator, I instinctively believe it is best that there be no sudden, radical, or complete change in one of the keystone institutions of our society. For the good of all involved, I believe it is essential that continuity and stability in our educational establishment remain uncompromised. Having made that statement, let me hasten to add that there are times when it is imperative that the process of evolution and transition be deliberately stimulated and accelerated; a time for what has been termed "managed evolution." In education, this is such a time.

Today, there are more "pieces strewn about us" than ever—still unassembled. The time has come for gathering these pieces and, with great care, fashioning a model of education that bridges the technology gap in the classroom and, most significantly, allows teachers to readily impact both sides of the brain—leaving no child behind.

ONE FINAL THOUGHT

For the past 50 years, billions of dollars have been spent to infuse schools with technology. The inability to translate this enormous, costly effort into higher test scores is a failure of major proportions. No amount of rhetoric can rationalize the fact that much was expected and little realized. This book continues with a thoughtful analysis of this failure as an essential first step toward closing the technology gaps in the classroom.

In an article published in *Education Week,* Bacchetti says it well: "Any time schools fail, they betray a child's potential."[23]

NOTES

1. Cohen, David K., *Technology in Education: Looking toward 2020.* Hillsdale, NJ: Lawrence Erlbaum, 1988, p. 241.

2. Reiser, Robert A., "Instructional Technology: A History," in *Instructional Technology: Foundations*, ed. Robert Gagne. Hillsdale, NJ: Lawrence Erlbaum, 1987, p. 13.

3. Benjamin Darrow, quoted in Cuban, Larry, *Teachers and Machines.* New York: Teachers College Press, 1986, pp. 61, 79.

4. Stanley Pogrow, quoted in Cuban, *Teachers and Machines*, p. 79.

5. Morrison, G., Ross, S., and O'Dell, J., "Applications of Research to the Design of Computer-Based Instruction," in *Instructional Technology: Past, Present, and Future,* ed. Gary Anglin. Englewood, CO: Libraries Unlimited, 1991, p. 188.

6. Thompson, James J., *Instructional Communication.* New York: American Book Company, 1969, p. 107.

7. Hood, Florence F., "Planning Changes in Education: Futuristic Trends and Images," in *Education: A Time for Decisions,* ed. Kathleen M. Redd and Arthur M. Harkins. Washington, DC: World Future Society, 1980, p. 46.

8. Perelman, Lewis J., "Learning Our Lesson," *Futurist.* Vol. 20, March/April 1986, p. 21.

9. Halal, William and Liebowitz, Jay, "Telelearning: The Multimedia Revolution in Education," *Futurist.* Vol. 28, November–December 1994, p. 21.

10. Carnegie Foundation for the Advancement of Teaching, *The Fourth Revolution: Instructional Technology in Higher Education.* Hightstown, NJ: McGraw-Hill, 1972, p. 9.

11. Carnegie Foundation, *Fourth Revolution,* p. 41.

12. U.S. Congress, Office of Technology Assessment, *Teachers and Technology: Making the Connection.* OTA-EHR-616. Washington, DC: U.S. Government Printing Office, 1995, p. iii.

13. Fisher, Charles, Dwyer, David, and Yocam, Keith, *Education and Technology.* San Francisco: Apple Press, 1996, p. xvi.

14. Thornburg, David B., *Education in the Communication Age*. San Carlos, CA: Thornburg and Starsong, 1994, p. 22.

15. Steinberg, Lawrence, *Beyond the Classroom: Why School Reform Has Failed*. New York: Simon and Schuster, 1996, p. 60.

16. McKim, R. H., *Experiences in Visual Thinking*. Monterey, CA: Brooks/ Cole, 1972, p. 9.

17. Williams, Linda V., *Teaching for the Two-Sided Mind*. New York: Simon and Schuster, 1983, p. 142.

18. Freed, Jeffrey, and Parsons, Laurie, *Right-Brained Children in a Left-Brained World*. New York: Simon and Schuster, 1998, p. 76.

19. Perelman, Lewis J., *School's Out*. New York: Avon, 1992.

20. Burkman, Ernest, "Factors Affecting Utilization," in *Instructional Technology: Foundations,* ed. Robert Gagne. Hillside, NJ: Lawrence Erlbaum, 1987, p. 445.

21. Reiser, Robert A., "Instructional Technology and Public Education in the United States," in *Instructional Communications,* ed. James Thompson. Englewood, CO: Libraries Unlimited, 1991, p. 219.

22. Bacchetti, Raymond, "Staying Power," *Education Week*. November 10, 1999, p. 48.

③

FIFTY YEARS OF UNREALIZED EXPECTATIONS

Without analyzing failure, one is, at best, groping for success.

—Michael T. Romano

About this chapter:

- It notes the value of analyzing the unrealized expectations of the past half century.
- It identifies the barriers to the effective use of technology in the classroom.
- It discusses the role of three major, legitimate vested interests in the education establishment.
- It analyzes the landmark Apple Classroom of Tomorrow project.

A LOOK BACK BEFORE MOVING AHEAD

"As a society, we squander the limited resources we have for innovation in education by overinvesting in the search for the next revolution and underinvesting in efforts to learn from the last one," says Decker F. Walker, professor of education, Stanford University.[1]

Dr. Walker is one of the education theorists involved with the landmark Apple Classroom of Tomorrow project. His statement supports my contention that without analyzing failure, one is, at best, groping for success.

BARRIERS TO THE EFFECTIVE USE OF TECHNOLOGY

In addressing why the technology gap in the classroom exists, six primary barriers to the effective use of technology by teachers have been identified:

1. After more than a half century of trial and error, it has been acknowledged at the highest level that there is still no common, coherent vision of how technology is to be used in the classroom; there are essentially only unrealized expectations.
2. Teachers have not been provided a convincing explanation of how technology would empower them. It has been erroneously perceived by some as a threat to their professional security rather than an amplification of their capacity to function.
3. At the highest level, there are misconceptions regarding the teacher's role in adapting technology to teaching and learning. How other professionals have been empowered with technology has not been considered.
4. The critical significance of course-specific software has not been understood. Most of the time, off-the-shelf software does not adequately integrate into the curriculum, thus rendering its effectiveness marginal.
5. In the past, there have been applications of technology in which results have been compromised by ill-conceived, incompatible utilization strategies. There has been little attempt to analyze and then profit from the many failures of the last 50 years.
6. There is ample evidence that leaders in education lack a full grasp of technology's capacity to make teaching and learning more effective and efficient. Consequently, their potential impact on promoting the use of technology is not fully realized.

DISCUSSION

These barriers to the effective use of technology by teachers serve as the basis for the application strategies brought forth later.

1. After more than a half century of trial and error, it has been acknowledged at the highest level that there is still no common, coherent vision of how technology is to be used in the classroom; there are only unrealized expectations.

Jacobson and Byrne offer this observation: "Education reform in past decades has involved multiple interventions, but a high level of incoherence."[2] This has been perceived by others and referred to as the need for a common, coherent vision.[3]

The 1995 federal legislation entitled "Goals 2000"[4] set a national agenda intended to propel American education into the twenty-first century. The section on educational technology must be viewed as authoritative, leading-edge thinking. It offers the following list of goals that are introduced with the statement: "The Goals 2000 Act provides leadership at the federal level, through the Department of Education by developing a national vision and strategy to:

- Promote awareness of the potential of technology for improving teaching and learning;
- demonstrate ways in which technology can be used to improve teaching and learning, and to help ensure that all students have an equal opportunity;
- ensure the availability and dissemination of knowledge that can be the basis for sound decisions about investment in, and effective uses of, educational technology;
- promote high-quality professional development opportunities for teachers and administrators regarding the integration of technology into instruction; and
- monitor advancements in technology to encourage the development of effective educational uses of technology."

These objectives set forth at the national level in 1995 clearly demonstrated that the United States was far from articulating a coherent, definitive approach to effectively empowering teachers with technology in spite of 50 years of costly trial and error. As noted in chapter 1, this conclusion is confirmed by a number of authoritative sources including the UNESCO International Congress on Infomatics in 1989;[5] the U.S. Congress Office of Technology Assessment in 1995;[6] the Apple Classroom of Tomorrow project in 1996;[7] and, the Milken Exchange on Educational Technology study in 1999.[8] Perhaps the most significant confirmation is the fact that in 2002, the U.S. Office of Education announced a three-year, $15 million study to determine "how technology is applied to the curriculum."[9]

Thus, regarding the question of why technology is not used routinely in classrooms, it is evident that, simply, *no one knows how to do it* in a manner that provides broad-scaled, quantifiable increases in learner achievement.

2. Teachers have not been provided a convincing explanation of how technology would empower them. It has been erroneously perceived by some as a threat to their professional security rather than an amplification of their capacity to function.

The Apple Classroom of Tomorrow project has defined the teacher's critical role in the use of technology as follows:

> The most important piece of hardware in the classroom isn't the multimedia computer, the video camera or the network. It's the teacher's desk, where any innovation must pass in one form or another before it gets to the students. The teacher isn't merely a gatekeeper; he or she is an orchestrator of the curriculum and will greatly influence how technology fits into the classroom.[10]

In a number of administrative capacities at the university level, I was involved for over three decades in encouraging teachers to take advantage of the costly technology placed at their disposal. Additionally, as part of the research for this book, 17 schools, from primary to graduate, were visited and 83 teachers interviewed. It can be reported that teachers:

- harbor a justifiable uneasiness that they might be replaced by an electronic terminal;
- generally have not been convinced of technology's potential to markedly amplify their capacity to function;

- instinctively resist anything or anyone intruding on the traditional sanctity of their classroom;
- appear to be locked into a seemingly rational mind-set: I function as proof that yesterday's approach to teaching works; therefore, if it worked for me, it will work for my learners; and
- have not been provided meaningful incentives to master new ways to function.

Godfrey expresses this rather critical opinion: "We naively believe that demonstrating the effectiveness of technology-based instruction will open the door to acceptance by teachers. Not at all; they will perceive it as a threat."[11]

The insecurity and anxiety displayed by some teachers regarding the use of technology has been fostered, to some extent, by a flow of thoughtless and questionable statements made over the decades. For example, as early as 1960, in this book, Heinich quotes Finn, an internationally prominent education guru, who said that educational technology had developed to the point where "it is now possible not only to replace the teacher, but also the entire school system."[12]

It is rational that anyone threatened with extinction must react defensively. Teachers cannot be exceptions. Thus, in 1970, the National Education Association (NEA, the teachers' union) made an overtly defensive position statement: "Teachers are autonomous professionals who can be trusted to make judgments about the needs and capabilities of their class. We must allow them to decide at what times and in what ways to utilize the entire armamentarium of devices and materials at their disposal, the newer learning media included."[13]

Then in 1997, facing the ever-growing push toward computer-based instruction, the NEA again made clear its position on the use of technology: "Instructional technology should be used to support instruction, but no reduction of positions, hours, or compensation should occur as a direct or indirect result of any technological programs."[14]

Still another aspect of this situation is the matter of incentives. Surgeons grasped immediately that a heart/lung machine would allow them to markedly increase the scope of the cardiopulmonary surgery they could perform. This benefited patients and, inevitably, surgeons' own stature. Unfortunately, nothing even remotely approaching this type of direct-line reward system exists for teachers.

An unusually candid statement by Albert Shanker, late president of the American Federation of Teachers, made this point amply clear. He said, as reported by Perelman, "I don't think you'd see technology used in business today if there were not consequences for not using it. It's used because firms have to use it; and, if they don't use it, they'll be out of business because somebody else is. And further, [technology] is going to do things more efficiently, and do them better. We don't have that situation in education."[15] It is my view that Mr. Shanker's understanding of the potential of technology in the classroom may be somewhat limited, because technology can allow teachers to do things better and more efficiently; it can—without a doubt—empower them as it has other professionals.

For example, a teacher empowered with technology producing video images can engage learners and escort them to the moon, to the bottom of the ocean, or inside a fertilized egg as it divides to create a new life. A teacher with only a chalkboard simply cannot. Also, a teacher providing learners access to a computer programmed with course-specific remedial tutoring is markedly more efficient than one trying to find time to provide one-on-one tutoring to each member of the class. This list of examples can be continued extensively.

Finally, the literature indicates that for decades teachers have been criticized by many for their apparent negative attitude toward accepting technology and innovation in general. The teachers' apparent resistance to change has been viewed as a ritualization of the long-standing, enduring books, chalkboard, and teacher-talk approach to education. Cohen has described a "popular culture of instruction that is old, deeply ingrained and powerful; a sea of popular, traditional practices of teaching and learning."[16]

After more than three decades of fostering the use of technology in education, I would propose that the key to dealing with the teachers' allegiance to the status quo is to convince them, beyond a shadow of a doubt, that technology will empower them with a new and greater capacity to do what they do—*better*. And, most important, that the change involved is well within their power to grasp and will not in any way compromise their traditional central role in the classroom. There is no evidence that a strategy for the use of technology in education has yet been proposed that directly addresses these critical requisites.

3. At the highest level, there are misconceptions regarding the teacher's role in adapting technology to teaching and learning. How other professionals have been empowered with technology has not been considered.

There is a long-standing mind-set that teachers require extensive training to effectively utilize technology. Further, it has been noted, "Teacher education programs in the United States do not prepare graduates to use technology as a teaching tool."[17]

A 1999 survey conducted for *Education Week* reported the most important obstacle inhibiting the use of technology by teachers is a lack of training. Further, a lack of time to prepare for its use is the second most frequently cited obstacle.[18]

In response to this situation, in fiscal year 2000, the U.S. Department of Education supported 86 programs related to training teachers in the use of technology. Since most exist as components of various larger programs, the specific amount of dollars involved cannot be determined. However, it is estimated to be between 2 and 3 billion dollars per year for the past decade.[19]

In 1992, the International Society for Technology in Education set forth 13 guidelines defining what teachers need to know to use technology. These have been approved by national accrediting agencies and include how to evaluate which computers and related technologies to use; apply instructional principles, research, and assessment practices; select, evaluate, and document the use of software; design and develop learning activities that integrate technology; and demonstrate knowledge of multimedia, hypermedia, and telecommunications.[20]

If, in fact, these are the requisites for the effective use of technology, then, as an educator, I believe that for most they are intimidating, unrealistic, anxiety provoking, and a major factor in rendering some teachers technophobic.

How can all of this be rationalized when it has been established—conclusively—that we still don't know how to use technology in the classroom? How can we possibly design effective training programs? What do we actually teach in these 86 federally funded programs costing billions? Here is an analysis of the vexing situation teachers face:

- They are pressured from many quarters to use technology; most teachers have been convinced that, in fact, they should use technology.

- They are concerned about what they are told they need to know in order to use technology.
- They are concerned about finding the time to learn all that they need to know.
- They are concerned about finding the time to actually integrate technology into their curricula—after they learn all that they need to know.
- And what is the most disconcerting, when they take the training programs, they come away without a clear-cut understanding of how to deal with all of these critical concerns.

Understandably, they return to their classrooms to teach in the same way they, their parents, and their grandparents were taught.

This is—without a doubt—a veritable catch-22 that needs to be addressed directly on a high-priority basis or we will continue to confound teachers while continuing to pour billions into a black hole. The key to getting beyond this intolerable impasse is to consider how other professionals have been empowered with technology and then apply the same basic, common-sense approach to teachers.

For example, physicians routinely integrate the CAT scan (computerized axial tomography) into their diagnostic techniques. They had no role in developing the basic technology, determining when its use is indicated or contraindicated, deciding the optimal exposures for different organs, judging how best to access different organs, or determining the criteria for interpreting the data produced. This had all been accomplished by others with highly specialized knowledge and skill.

Additionally, critical to the initial development of this valuable diagnostic tool was the requirement that its integration into the treatment room be as user-friendly as possible. Thus, the training programs for those who perform the scan and those who interpret the data had to be compatible in terms of their existing knowledge level and time constraints.

This reality-based approach is used in the introduction of new technology everywhere—except education. In this context, the guidelines listed earlier for what teachers need to know set forth by the International Society for Technology in Education must be viewed as unrealistic and essentially counterproductive.

4. The critical significance of course-specific software has not been understood. Most of the time, off-the-shelf software does not adequately integrate into the curriculum, thus rendering its effectiveness marginal.

What is a curriculum? Pilots have flight plans. Physicians have treatment plans. Coaches have game plans. Teachers have curricula. A curriculum is a strategy put in place that specifies what to teach, when to teach it, and how to teach it. It is not arbitrary; it is specific. It has time constraints; thus, it has little flexibility. Finally, the teacher's capacity to manage it, in great part, determines the outcome of the teaching-learning process.

A curriculum is driven by information. Determined by specific learning objectives, the information is carefully selected and precisely sequenced. All of this planning is based on the predetermined game plan. Finding computer software that exactly fits a slot in the curriculum is a formidable chore.

Additionally, it is pertinent to note that for centuries the primary medium in education has been print. At all levels, there is a support system in place to provide printed materials of all varieties: handouts, manuals, and textbooks. Again, it has been accepted that to maintain the integrity of the curriculum, all of these must be specific to what is being taught.

Following this age-old precedent, it is essential that we do with the newer information technology what has been done with print: provide teachers the support system necessary to create course-specific software. Teachers' role in this new support system must be based on a realistic appraisal of their knowledge, skills, and time constraints. Anything less will compromise the realization of technology's full potential.

This view is confirmed by a number of sources. Perhaps the most authoritative is the 10-year Apple Classroom of Tomorrow study, which reported: "Technology alone cannot improve teaching and learning. Technology use must be grounded firmly in curriculum goals, incorporated in a sound instructional process, and deeply integrated with subject matter content. Absent this grounding, that too often is neglected in the rush to glittery application, changes in student performance are unlikely."[21]

This conclusion is supported by many other reliable sources including the International Society for Technology in Education, in collaboration with the U.S. Department of Education;[22] the Milken Exchange on Education Technology;[23] the U.S. Congress Office of Technology Assessment;[24] and the *Education Week* study in collaboration with the Milken Exchange.[25]

What is difficult to rationalize is that the focus and funding continues to be for hardware and off-the-shelf software. There is enough evidence to begin supporting the development of teacher-support systems to produce course-specific software as we have done for print. Admittedly, this is a formidable, costly task, but it is not without precedent.

In the 1960s, education placed its hope for improving learner achievement on the use of television. Then, academic institutions at all levels developed TV production facilities. Some were at a level of sophistication equal to their commercial counterparts. Their mission was to create course-specific video, and many did it superbly. Why educational television did not produce the anticipated results is pertinent to what is happening today with computers and is explored in chapter 5.

Still another analogy is the systems developed to support other professionals in order to optimally empower them with technology. An example is the surgeon who in 1950 removed gallbladders and now transplants hearts. The system required to get the donor's heart to the recipient at the operating table is understandably complex and costly—but essential.

Finally, the matter of the Internet needs to be included in this discussion. Supported by the federal government, billions are being spent to bring this potentially powerful information resource to every classroom. Again, the critical matter of curriculum-specific information must be reconciled. In a 1999 study, teachers noted, "It is too difficult and time-consuming to find appropriate Web sites, preview them and develop materials to bring them into lessons."[26] How teachers and learners might manage the overwhelming amount of "unprocessed" information delivered by the Internet had not been thoroughly thought through before the billions were spent; this is addressed subsequently in this book.

5. In the past, there have been applications of technology in which results have been compromised by ill-conceived, incompatible utilization strategies. There has been little attempt to analyze and then profit from the many failures of the last 50 years.

In the 1950s, there was the promise that a television monitor in every classroom, connected to an educational television (ETV) network, would improve and equalize the quality of education for all. Today, educational television is viewed by most to be a failed medium in the classroom because it has not met the ambitious goals defined 50 years ago.[27]

The ETV networks were created primarily to deliver electronically a competent teacher to every classroom deemed to be in need. Inevitably, it raised the specter of replacing live teachers with surrogates—images appearing on a cathode-ray tube. Understandably, it was anxiety provoking to the classroom gatekeepers—teachers. Further, it raised such questions as the following:

- Who decided which classroom teachers had to be bolstered by a television teacher and what criteria were used?
- Were there adequate attempts to inform the classroom teacher regarding what the television teachers would teach?
- Were the televised lessons compatible with the content and sequencing of the curriculum in place?
- How did classroom teachers feel when they relinquished their role to a televised teacher and sat in the back of the room?

These critical questions were not resolved to the satisfaction of all parties involved before the millions were spent. Stated another way, the compatibility factor was not considered in devising the utilization strategy for educational television.

Today, we have computers and the Internet, and a new set of questions that must be addressed:

- How many teachers are computer-literate?
- Can those who are not effectively integrate computers into their curricula?
- Is there sufficient understanding regarding precisely how to effectively integrate computers into the existing teaching-learning process?
- Do teachers and learners have the capacity to manage the deluge of information delivered to their classrooms by the Internet?

- What is the value of a bounteous supply of information if it is not processed into the curriculum?
- Is there an authoritative source with answers to these critical questions? Where? Who? When will that source come forth?

Based on a 50-year perspective, if these questions are not resolved in a forthright manner, the tremendous potential of computers and the Internet to empower teachers and improve learner achievement may not be fully realized.

Now, consider the case of motion pictures. Since their educational debut in the 1920s, their use has followed the pattern of the movie theater: the classroom had to be dark, no one dared to speak during the showing, and, once started, the film had to be shown in its entirety. Couldn't the classroom be moderately dark, so the teacher could stand beside the screen and keep eye contact with the learners? Couldn't the film be stopped at intervals, so the teacher and learners could discuss content and interact? Why couldn't the sound be off, with the teacher providing the narration? Couldn't selected segments be viewed as part of a lesson? All of this would have adapted film to the classroom rather than adapting the classroom to the movie theater.

Finally, the classic example of faulty technology application is the case of the slide-tape/study carrel. In the late 1960s, the audiocassette made its entry onto the scene. It soon became the new star on the electronic information stage. It had a major limitation, however—no picture.

This was, of course, a minor challenge to a nation on the verge of landing a man on the moon. Thus, in a rush to create profits, commercial entrepreneurs quickly developed the synchronized, rear-projection, slide-tape desktop unit. So now, an illustrated lecture, neatly and inexpensively packaged and retrievable on an individualized basis, was available.

This feat was quickly followed by a companion creation—the study carrel, a home base for the rear-projection unit. In schools throughout the land, large spaces were dedicated to the latest educational enchantment—self-study halls. These spaces were designed in an egg-crate configuration in which individual learners could sit, see a still picture, and hear the synchronized narration on earphones. This was a king-sized blunder on the part of entrepreneurs, aided and abetted by the educational establishment. No one took the time to think through the fallacy of this approach.

Slides were developed originally to allow large groups to simultaneously view a photographic print. If the objective was to provide the image solely to an individual, why didn't we simply revert back to a print? A print requires no rear-screen projection unit. A packet of prints and a portable audiocassette player would provide the same information retrieval system for a fraction of the cost. In addition, the retrieval mode, being completely portable, requires no carrel, thus eliminating the barrier of scheduling. Of course, study carrels with slide-tape units have long since quietly vanished from the scene.

A search of the literature reveals no evidence of any significant in-depth analysis of past failures. Many valuable lessons have been overlooked, and this has been a major detriment to the effective utilization of technology.

6. There is ample evidence that the leaders in education lack a full grasp of technology's capacity to make teaching and learning more effective and efficient. Consequently, their potential impact on promoting the use of technology is not fully realized.

In the Carnegie Commission report of 1972, the second recommendation stated that to ensure the advancement of educational technology, responsibility for its introduction and use "should be placed squarely on the shoulders of those at the highest possible level."[28] That was in 1972; today, there is ample evidence to indicate that those "at the highest possible level" are still not focused sharply on the potential of technology.

In 1995, a lay magazine interviewed the sitting U.S. secretary of education, Richard Riley, regarding his prescription for preparing the country's educational system for the twenty-first century.[29] The initiative, he noted, consisted of attaining the objectives listed in the 1994 legislative act Goals 2000.

The act does include a technology proposal; yet, in this lengthy interview, the secretary makes no mention or intimation that, as a high priority, schools need to be made as technology-dependent as the world beyond their walls. It can only be assumed his understanding of the potential of technology is somewhat marginal.

Additionally, the national commission members that issued the alarming *Nation at Risk* report in 1983 were, for the most part, academic administrators.[30] They brought forth five recommendations intended to reform our educational system. None of them referred to the critical technology gap in the classroom. Further, although they noted nine "essential raw materials needed to reform our (ailing) educational system— waiting to be mobilized through effective leadership," there was no mention of technology.

Then, in 1998, a commissioner in the U.S. Department of Education issued a lengthy statement about the lack of improvement in our children's scholastic achievement since the 1983 *Nation at Risk* report.[31] In the 1997 Third International Mathematics and Science Study (TIMSS), commenting on the dismal U.S. performance, he said, "TIMSS data do encourage us to focus on rigorous content, focused curriculum, and good teaching as critical to improved national performance." It is my opinion that, in fact, this type of musty thinking at the highest level has contributed to placing this nation at risk.

This analysis of the six primary barriers to effectively empowering teachers with technology indicates they are real and, indeed, formidable. However, to move beyond the present circumstances they undoubtedly must be addressed. The first step has been taken—they have been identified.

THE ROLE OF MAJOR VESTED INTERESTS

To obtain a broad understanding of the forces that shape U.S. education, the research for this book has included interviews with individuals from three major, legitimate vested interests in the education establishment: the assistant to the director of Educational Technology at the U.S. Department of Education; the director of the Technology Center at the National Education Association; and a vice president at IBM directing its multimillion-dollar Reinventing Education Program.

Recognizing the impact these three powerful entities have on education, I decided to seek answers to the following questions: What is their vision regarding technology and education? Are they collaborating to maximize the enormous power they wield? Are they heeding the lessons of past failures? How well are they succeeding in reconciling their self-interest with what is best for *empowering teachers with technology* and improving how our youth learn?

A summary of their input is reported in the following sections. Although several points have previously been noted, they are significant and warrant repetition.

The U.S. Department of Education

The multibillion-dollar effort to support the use of educational technology has been driven since 1994 primarily by three goals: train teachers to use technology, increase support of research on how to use technology, and connect all classrooms to the Internet. All appear to be desirable goals. However, we failed to ascertain from our discussion with the department adequate answers to some crucial questions:

- Acknowledging the need to invest in research on how to use technology, what expectations do you have regarding the actual content of the costly teacher-training programs you fund if we still don't know how best to use technology?
- Have you determined the extent to which the research you have funded over the past half century has been applied in the classroom?
- What guidance will you provide teachers and learners on how to integrate into their curricula the "oceans" of unprocessed information to be delivered to their classrooms by the Internet?
- Have you determined why a TV monitor in every classroom connected to a costly ETV network in the 1960s failed to meet the expectations of improved learning?
- What assurances can you make that computers and the Internet will succeed?
- Do you have a strategy to overcome teachers' justifiable concern about being replaced by an electronic terminal?

Were these critical questions addressed before the billions were committed to teacher training, research, and the Internet?

The National Education Association

The union exists as a major force in education, dedicated to safeguarding the status of its members—teachers. Indeed, this is a legitimate, vested interest. Its Resolutions B-60, B-61, and B-62, passed by the membership at the 1997 annual meeting, set forth its position regarding the use of technology with uncommon candor.[32] Following are excerpts:

- Instructional technology should be used to support instruction, but no reduction of positions, hours, or compensation should occur as a direct or indirect result of any technological programs.
- Education employees should be provided encouragement, time, and resources to experiment with and to research applications of technology in order to integrate technology into the curriculum.
- Education employees, including representatives of the local association, must be involved in all aspects of technology utilization, including planning, materials selection, implementation, and evaluation.
- Ongoing training must be provided in the use of technologies and applications; teacher preparation in instructional technology, including the development of effective materials and the appropriate instructional strategies, must begin in college and extend through continuing professional development.

In addition to these key resolutions, more statements can be cited that provide insight into the NEA's position regarding the use of technology in the classroom:

- It created the NEA Center for Education Technology "to be sure that technology truly does benefit the teaching and learning process and to put the NEA and its affiliates at the cutting edge."[33]
- A technology brief published by the center stated: "If technology is to achieve its ultimate use in the classroom, what teachers know is of prime concern. At least 50% of today's teachers have not had adequate training and technical assistance in the use of technology."[34]
- In 1997, Robert Chase, president of the NEA, said, "We see communication technology, in the hands of educators trained to use it, as a marvelous new learning tool that will improve the quality of education—but, we also see the possibility of technology being used to devalue our product. It can put more teachers out of students' reach."[35]

Although this analysis of the NEA's posture regarding technology and education was limited, it did surface a number of critical questions:

- Does the teacher's acknowledged lack of understanding regarding how to use technology undermine the NEA's recommendation that teachers be involved in "all planning for its use in the classroom"?
- How does the NEA reconcile its support for additional research on the use of technology and the effectiveness of teacher-training programs?
- If technology increases the teacher's capacity to function—as it has for other professionals—would it not increase teachers' intrinsic value to society?

Contact with the association did not provide an understanding of how it is addressing these cogent issues.

IBM Corporation

Major corporations are understandably concerned about the educational achievement of young people joining the workforce. Thus, IBM has initiated a multimillion-dollar program entitled "Reinventing Education." Its aim: "To push reform beyond individual school buildings—to transform entire school districts and state education systems, thus paving the way to a completely new system of public education with higher standards and improved student performance."[36]

Discussing this program, the vice president directing it expressed the view that what teachers do in the classroom is outmoded and must be completely changed. Unfortunately, discussions with IBM were not adequate to determine whether it had answers to the following critical questions:

- If you succeed in creating a "completely new system of public education," how would you dismantle the existing system?
- How would the two powerful teachers' unions react to rendering their teachers' skills and work patterns obsolete?
- Have you studied the 10-year Apple Classroom of Tomorrow failure? What will you do that it did not do?

Unless these questions are approached directly and answered to the satisfaction of all parties involved, there is the risk that IBM will dump *additional* millions into the abyss of educational technology utilization, despite commendable intentions.

Viewed retrospectively, it appears there is little meaningful collaboration between the powerful parties discussed here. Also, there is little historical perspective to help shape their vision. There are, however, extremely commendable intentions, much effort put forth by cadres of dedicated professionals, a great deal of rhetoric, and large sums of money committed to helping teachers integrate technology into what happens in the classroom. Nonetheless, test scores indicate there has been no meaningful, quantifiable impact on learner achievement.

ANALYZING THE LANDMARK ACOT PROJECT

The Apple Classroom of Tomorrow (ACOT) project was an ambitious, unprecedented effort to demonstrate the optimal application of computers to teaching and learning. Initiated in 1986 by the Apple Computer Corporation, it involved some of the nation's finest education theorists supported by substantial financial resources.

In 1986, at five sites throughout the United States, one classroom in each school was "saturated" with computer technology. This included a personal computer for each learner and teacher in the class and a companion unit at home. The goal was to develop the most effective approach to utilizing computer technology and then have that technology-enriched classroom serve as a model for others.

In 1989, the number of sites was reduced from five to three. Then, in 1996, 10 years and undisclosed millions of dollars later, a book was published that documented the decade-long ACOT experience.[37] This landmark discourse on computers and education has to be considered authoritative and timely. It acknowledges—quite candidly—that "ACOT failed to deliver the revolution everybody wanted" (p. 98).

An analysis of this failure is pertinent to this discussion. Here are some excerpts from the ACOT report (all italics added):

- American educators have had more than a decade in which to learn from our pioneering experiments with the use of computers.

What have we learned? *Not as much* as we could have, or should have . . . (p. 92)

- The use of computers demands changes in deeply held beliefs about the respective roles of teachers and students, the goals of education, the very concept of knowledge, and the means to measure student success. (p. 16)
- The set beliefs around lecture-dominated instruction are formally sanctioned when new teachers arrive at their schools, by administrators and in the faculty lounge by other teachers. This explains the *intransigence* of traditional schooling to change. In the end, teachers most likely teach as they were taught. (p. 19)
- In our own naïveté, we had no idea about the *system-changing forces* we were about to unleash. Sometimes the expectations seemed too much, and teachers worried about getting through the year and covering the basics. (p. 22)
- Simplicity is hard when opportunities are many. Many uses of computers are too flexible and general. Most students and teachers would do better with a *few* concrete and simple things. (p. 76)
- As you use the computer, you start questioning everything you have done in the past, and wonder how you can adapt it to the computer. (p. 24)
- The strategy of designing and implementing new models of education in a few places, and then reproducing them elsewhere *does not work at all well* for broad change in education. (p. 37)
- Schools of education are little altered to reflect changed ideas about digital education; we are asking teachers to do *radically* redesigned jobs. (p. 44)
- How awkwardly computers fit into schools. We could only fit seven of them in a classroom, and even then, there was not enough room for students to work together. (p. 59)
- Technology use *must be grounded firmly in curriculum goals,* incorporated in sound instructional process. (p. 200)
- If we had renewed our commitment to *teacher-centered,* close-to-the-classroom innovation, I think the results would have been much more impressive. (p. 99)
- No one has an incentive to *look back, to study failures,* to salvage what worked, to fix what didn't and to avoid making the same mistake next time. (p. 97)

- In this maze of reform efforts, *the role of technology in education remains unclear* even as it is championed (or denounced) by contending voices. (p. vii)

It is this investigator's conclusion that the ACOT effort failed to meet expectations because it did not heed the lessons of the past 50 years: as has been noted several times, *there can be no revolutions in education;* change must be evolutionary. The new must be adapted with great care to what exists or the system will reject it. It is a situation where *less is more.*

Hypothetically, if a new country with unlimited resources were being created, and a new educational system was being developed from the ground up, the ACOT concept might succeed. But today in the United States, there exists a vast, entrenched system with established operational patterns, century-old teaching methods, a myriad of venerable curricula, a battery of national and local evaluation instruments, colleges of education with traditional curricula, teachers' unions, and established book publishers, facilities, and financial support mechanisms. Undoubtedly, with these constraints in place, the ACOT revolution faced formidable obstacles. Specifically, this analysis of the ACOT experience has led to the following conclusions:

- Not enough teachers can adapt to radically redesigned operational patterns. Over the years, most efforts to retrain teachers on a broad-scaled basis have failed. Thus, the increment of change must be carefully measured in order to be readily assimilated by teachers.
- Most teachers have not been trained to do research. Even if they were, meeting their teaching obligations must be given priority.
- The search for off-the-shelf, curriculum-specific software was time-consuming and disruptive for both teachers and learners. A curriculum must be negotiated within a given time frame; thus, the availability of course materials must conform to a predetermined critical sequence.
- Existing school facilities can only accommodate a certain number of computers. The saturation approach prescribed by ACOT presents a virtually insurmountable space obstacle. Obviously, it is not

feasible to create enough Apple Classrooms of Tomorrow in today's schools.

- The cost of two computers per student—one in class and one at home—is prohibitive. A relatively poor state such as Kentucky has 639,579 students in its K–12 public school system. At a cost of $2,000 per person, the initial cost would be over $1.2 billion. What of upkeep? Replacement? Cost of software?

The strategy of model development and dissemination has a long history of failure because a new model—*compatible with the system in place*—that produces a significant, dramatic increase in learner achievement has not been developed. If that time comes, there is reason to believe there will be enough external pressure on the system to force broad-scaled adoption.

Indeed, much has been learned from the ACOT project. Above all else, it confirmed what has been experienced by many other would-be innovators over the past 50 years. The compatibility factor is real and is formidable. The new must be linked to the old or there can be no meaningful change in education. The *Technology-Enhanced Curriculum* described in the following chapters is carefully designed to deal directly with all these critical factors.

ONE FINAL THOUGHT

Understandably, this chapter represents the author's perception of reality. To preserve the integrity of the work, it has been necessary to be somewhat critical of the efforts of some in the education establishment. Let it be clear there is no intention to impugn motives but, rather, to raise questions regarding their perception of a profoundly intricate matter.

NOTES

1. Fisher, Charles, Dwyer, David, and Yocam, Keith, *Education and Technology*. San Francisco: Apple Press, 1996, p. 97.

2. Jacobson, Stephen and Byrne, Robert, *Reforming Education: The Emerging Systemic Approach.* Thousand Oaks, CA: Sage, 1993, p. 85.

3. Cornish, Edward, foreword, in *Education: A Time for Decisions,* ed. Kathleen M. Redd and Arthur M. Harkins. Washington, DC: World Future Society, 1980, p. v; Gilbert, Steven, "Making the Most of a Slow Revolution," *Change.* March/April 1996, p. 23; U.S. Congress, Office of Technology Assessment, *Teachers and Technology: Making the Connection.* OTA-EHR-616, Washington, DC: U.S. Government Printing Office, 1995, p. 127.

4. U.S. Congress, OTA, *Teachers and Technology,* p. 220.

5. Ely, Donald P., "Trends and Issues in Educational Technology," in *Instructional Technology: Past, Present, and Future,* ed. Gary Anglin. Englewood, CO: Libraries Unlimited, 1991, p. 50.

6. U.S. Congress, OTA, *Teachers and Technology,* p. 125.

7. Fisher, Dwyer, and Yocam, *Education and Technology,* p. xvi.

8. Fatemi, Erik, ed., "Building the Digital Curriculum," in *Technology Counts '99,* supplement to *Education Week.* September 23, 1999, p. 6.

9. Trotter, Andrew, "Department Study to Examine Effectiveness of Technology," *Education Week.* February 6, 2002, p. 23.

10. Fisher, Dwyer, and Yocam, *Education and Technology,* p. 207.

11. Godfrey, Eleanor, "Restructuring, Technology, and Instructional Productivity," in *Instructional Technology: Past, Present, and Future,* ed. Gary Anglin. Englewood, CO: Libraries Unlimited, 1991, p. 237.

12. Finn quoted in Heinich, Robert, "The Proper Study of Instructional Technology," in *Instructional Technology: Past, Present, and Future,* ed. Gary Anglin. Englewood, CO: Libraries Unlimited, 1991, p. 68.

13. Heinich, Robert, *Technology and the Management of Instruction.* Bloomington, IN: Association for Educational Technology and Communication, 1970, p. 46.

14. Center for Education Technology, *Technology Brief No. 10.* Washington, DC: National Education Association, 1997, pp. 1–2.

15. Perelman, Lewis J., *School's Out.* New York: Avon, 1992, p. 154.

16. Cohen, David K., *Technology in Education: Looking toward 2020.* Hillsdale, NJ: Lawrence Erlbaum, 1988, p. 250.

17. U.S. Congress, OTA, *Teachers and Technology,* p. 184.

18. Fatemi, "Building the Digital Curriculum," p. 7.

19. U.S. Congress, OTA, *Teachers and Technology,* p. 29.

20. U.S. Congress, OTA, *Teachers and Technology,* p. 177.

21. Fisher, Dwyer, and Yocam, *Education and Technology,* p. 200.

22. International Society for Technology in Education, *The National Educational Technology Standards for Students: Connecting Curriculum and Technology.* Eugene, OR: ISTE, 2000, p. 28.

23. Coughlin, Edward and Lemke, Cheryl, *Professional Skills for the Digital Age Classroom.* Santa Monica, CA: Milken Exchange on Education Technology, 1999, p. 23.

24. U.S. Congress, OTA, *Teachers and Technology*, p. 130.

25. Jerald, C. and Orlofsky, G., "Raising the Bar on School Technology," in *Technology Counts '99*, supplement to *Education Week.* September 23, 1999, p. 62.

26. Lehr, M., "Screening for the Best," in *Technology Counts '99*, supplement to *Education Week.* September 23, 1999, p. 19.

27. Cambre, Marjorie, "The State of the Art of Instructional Television," in *Instructional Technology: Past, Present, and Future*, ed. Gary Anglin. Englewood, CO: Libraries Unlimited, 1991, p. 267; Cohen, *Technology in Education*, p. 253; Thompson, J., *Instructional Communication.* New York: American Book Company, 1969, p. 107.

28. Carnegie Foundation for the Advancement of Teaching, *The Fourth Revolution: Instructional Technology in Higher Education.* Hightstown, NJ: McGraw-Hill, 1972, p. 43.

29. Winik, Lyric, "We Are Responsible," in *Parade Magazine.* March 19, 1995, p. 6.

30. *A Nation at Risk: The Imperative for Educational Reform.* Washington, DC: U.S. Government Printing Office, No. 065-000-00177-2, 1983.

31. Forgione, Pascal, "Achievement in the United States: Progress Since a Nation at Risk?" *NCES World Wide Home Page.* www.nces.ed.gov (accessed April 3, 1998).

32. Center for Education Technology, *Technology Brief No. 10*, pp. 1–2.

33. Center for Education Technology, brochure. Washington, DC: National Education Association, 1996, p. 2.

34. Center for Education Technology, *Technology Brief No. 11.* Washington, DC: 1997, p. 1.

35. Chase, Robert, "The New NEA: Reinventing Teacher Unions for a New Era." Paper presented to the National Press Club, Washington, DC, February 5, 1997.

36. International Business Machines Corporation, *Reinventing Education*, brochure. Armonk, NY: Corporate Support Programs, IBM, 1996, p. 3.

37. Fisher, Dwyer, and Yocam, *Education and Technology*, p. 100.

4

THE INFORMATION AGE
AND WHAT TEACHERS DO

Information is the fuel that powers the teaching-learning process.

—Michael T. Romano

About this chapter:

- It is structured around a series of interrelated perceptions.
- It introduces the concept of how humans amplify their capacity to function.
- It provides an overview of the Information Age and its potential impact on teaching and learning.
- It notes the role of sensory perceptions in learning and the development of the individual.
- It discusses the fundamentals of information management in relation to how a teacher functions.
- It offers an analysis of what teachers do and how information technology can *empower them so they might do it better.*

WHAT WE KNOW AND WHAT WE DON'T KNOW

Of course, everyone knows what teachers do. A global society is emerging, catalyzed by the Information Age—because of what teachers do. We went to the moon—because of what teachers do. We transplant hearts—because of what teachers do. Ironically, we have created the means to have them do what they do better—far better—and yet, we still *don't know how* to fashion a lasting bond between teachers and the incredible information technology that is transforming society around the globe.

The ultimate *Digital Age curriculum* to be brought forth was conceived by analyzing what teachers do and what technology does, and then carefully integrating the two. To appreciate the validity of the concept it is necessary to understand the core information technologies, television and computers, and how they provide teachers the capacity to more effectively manage information. Hence the objectives of the next three chapters.

AMPLIFYING HUMAN CAPACITY: A BASIC CONCEPT

Perception

Human progress from the Stone Age to the Information Age resulted primarily from amplifying individuals' capacity to function, first by empowering them with crude implements, then tools, then machines, and now technology. This is basic to understanding how teachers can do what they do—better.

Ralph Waldo Emerson noted in 1850 that all tools and engines on earth are only extensions of humankind's limbs and senses. Philosopher Samuel Butler added that the history of man is, in great part, a continuing account of the extension of his senses.[1] How does today's sophisticated information technology impact the human sensorium?

Dierker refers to a fascinating concept offered by McKeefrey, who speculates that the impact of a given technology can be quantified by determining the extent to which it multiplies human capacity *alone* to accomplish the same task.[2] For instance, considering a person can walk 4 miles per hour, an automobile traveling 60 miles per hour represents a 15-fold multiplier. A jet airplane at 600 miles per hour is a 150-fold multiplier.

The steam engine was a 1,000-fold multiplier, and it brought the Industrial Revolution. According to McKeefrey, human history experienced a million-fold multiplier only three times. The first was in communications; initially by wire and then by wireless, our ability to send messages, and thus conquer distance, has been amplified a millionfold. The second was nuclear energy, the total impact of which is still undetermined. The third was the computer. He speculates, "With the convergence of computers, linked to world-wide distribution technologies, we will, for the first time, *have a million-fold multiplication of a million-fold amplifier."*

McKeefrey notes that if a 100-fold amplifier brought about the Agricultural Revolution, and a 1,000-fold amplifier caused the Industrial Revolution, the implications of a million-fold multiplication of a million-fold amplifier are indeed too awesome to contemplate.

How much amplification of a teacher's capacity to function is narrating over a video of the moon landing, compared with a narration using only the aid of a chalkboard? Our approach to understanding the capacity of technology to empower teachers is based on McKeefrey's concept.

INFORMATION, HUMAN CAPACITY, AND EDUCATION

Perception

All human activity is driven by information; the more demanding the activity—the greater the need for information. Thus, information can be termed the fuel *that powers the teaching-learning process.*

Today, humans exist in an information-dependent society; a society that is hopelessly dysfunctional without a never-ceasing infusion of information. Thus, a general understanding of how information is managed at the broad, as well as the personal, level is useful in appreciating the connection between information technology, what teachers do, and how they can do it *better.*

In the broadest context, some view the advances in global networking as "arteries of mass communication."[3] Actually, it is more as though a *sensorium* for a global society has evolved. The television and computer distribution networks are the nervous system. The vast banks of computers strategically situated throughout the globe serve as the brain. The worldwide, news-gathering networks (for example, CNN) serve as the eyes and ears. Poised to function literally at the speed of light, these elements linked together serve the world as the human sensorium serves the individual; specifically, to provide information—the lifeblood, the fuel for all human activity.

Thompson took this concept farther when he considered the human organism to be a living, breathing communications system, continuously in the process of receiving and transmitting information.[4] He notes, "You are today the sum total of all the information you have ever acquired, which you consciously (or unconsciously) summon up to help you make decisions and, literally, to function." Thus, your behavior, your opinions, and your skills are all the sum total of the information you've processed throughout your life. Now, its pertinence to education.

Perception

At a fundamental level, it can be assumed that all learning is initiated by information perceived by the senses: specifically, what you see, hear, taste, smell, and feel.

Houston, an internationally recognized sociobiologist, concludes that as individuals develop from infancy, their progress—in great part— depends upon the development of their sensory perceptions.[5] Relating this to learning, it can be assumed that, in general, computer-generated, interactive multimedia vastly heightens sensory perceptions compared with those provided by books, chalkboard, and teacher-talk.

Perception

Information technology empowers teachers by amplifying their capacity to readily provide their learners the heightened *sensory perceptions of multimedia.*

THE INFORMATION AGE: AN OVERVIEW

The twentieth century came to a close, literally, with an explosion—an explosion of information. The Information Age is upon us with all its profound implications for the *tempo* of human progress. Thornburg said it best: "The info-genie is out of the bottle!"[6] Moreover, it can be perceived as knocking persistently on the door of the classroom.

Considering the information-intensive nature of education, there can be no doubt that the opportunities for teachers and learners are significant. To understand this monumental development, the Information Age should be considered first in the broadest context:

What is the incredible Information Age?

- It is the exploding capacity to create, transmit, and transform information with technologies that become exponentially smaller and smaller, faster and faster, cheaper and cheaper, more user-friendly, and ever so prolific and universal.[7]
- Projected into the new millennium, the Information Age will permit us to communicate and interrelate from our homes and businesses with anyone, anywhere, anytime. This is the capacity that will propel us to the next stage in the development of humankind—the Global Village.[8]
- While the shift from an agricultural to an industrial society took 100 years, the present restructuring from an industrial to an information society took only two decades.[9]
- In 1992, Perelman noted that in 1972 it would have taken 5 trillion human clerks to manually perform the calculations done by the world's then-current population of computers. With the great expansion of the power and number of computers, the hypothetical number of clerks in 1992 would be 100,000 times greater.[10]
- The national telecommunications policy is now focused on the replacement of copper wires with the glass threads of fiber-optic cables. Transmitting the entire contents of the Library of Congress over copper would take about 2,000 years. With fiber optics, at 8 million bits per second, the same result could be accomplished in eight hours.[11]

Perception

The master teachers of the Information Age are those who develop the capacity to navigate the worldwide oceans of information and selectively retrieve that which can provide an enriched experience for their learners.

Is there a downside to the remarkable Information Age?

- Naisbitt has warned: "People who do not educate themselves—and keep reeducating themselves—to participate in the new knowledge environment will be the *peasants* of the information society."[12]
- Not everyone is awed by the mind-boggling Information Age. Stoll remarked, somewhat cynically, that the key ingredient of *silicon snake oil* is a technocratic belief that computers and networks will make a better society.[13]

In spite of these conjectures, this much is certain: the *info-genie* is out of the bottle and is a force with which to contend. It is on par with the other mighty forces that have come before it—fire, steam, electricity, and nuclear energy. The challenge is to harness it—or *manage* it—so that it becomes a catalyst for the development of society in general, and teaching and learning specifically. Thus far, its impact on society is far beyond its impact on education.

THE FUNDAMENTALS OF INFORMATION MANAGEMENT

Information management has emerged as a science with its own name—*infomatics*. What follows is an elemental overview of this complex discipline, intended to provide a background for appreciating the core information technologies—television and computers and their potential to markedly amplify a teacher's capacity to function.

What Is Information?

Information is anything that can be seen, heard, smelled, tasted, or felt by the human sensorium. Each input of information stimulates or impacts the mind and causes a reaction. The individual may respond in a wide variety of ways or merely store the information in the mind for future use. Up to a point, the greater the number of inputs, the greater the impact on the mind. Beyond a point, too many inputs cause overload, which often short-circuits the mind. Some speculate the Internet presents this hazard to learners at the lower levels.

What Does "Managing" Information Mean?

It refers to harvesting and then converting information into a form suitable for transmission and immediate reception or storage for subsequent reception. Conveying verbal information to one person standing next to you does not require managing. Speaking to an audience of 100 in the same room requires amplification or management of the information. Managing information is central to what teachers do.

What Are the Basic Components of Information Management?

There are four: the sender, the receiver, the message, and the medium. The sender is the source of the message. The receiver is the interpreter, or the recipient, of the message. The message is an ordered set of symbols, the meaning of which is clear only from the reaction of each receiver. The medium is the carrier or conveyor of the message. In education, the teacher is the primary sender and the learner is the receiver. The selection of the medium—based on the message—is central to the outcome.

What Are "Replicas" and "Referents"?

A *replica* is a substitute for something that can be seen or heard, called the *referent*. Examples of replicas: the sound emanating from a speaker, the image on a television screen, a printed page, and so forth. In education, the disparity between the referent and the replica determines the *fidelity* of the information provided to the learner and is a major factor in determining the efficiency of the teaching-learning process.

Perception

How teachers manage information has a major impact on the outcome *of the teaching-learning process. Technology facilitates and amplifies the teacher's capacity to provide learners with information of* higher
fidelity *in an individualized, interactive mode. Thompson said that the
successful teacher primarily manages information, not students.*[14]

WHAT TEACHERS DO

Again, everyone knows *what teachers do.* It is ironic, therefore, that humans have come from the Stone Age to the Digital Age learning from each
other and that, apparently, there is still no generally accepted definition of
the teaching-learning process in the literature. Here are four views:

- Percival and Ellington: The process of education and learning can
  be considered to be a very complex system indeed.[15]
- Gagne: The systematic study of the phenomenon of human learning along with the accompanying theory development has had a
  somewhat schizophrenic history.[16]
- Fuhrman and Grasha: There is no simple theory of learning that
  will account for the complexity of the classroom-learning environment. The goal of developing a unified learning theory is desirable,
  but such a thing does not exist today.[17]
- Perelman: There may be no more common and erroneous stereo-
  type than the image of instruction as injecting knowledge into an
  empty head. The teacher faces the learner, taking on the critical
  role of "fountain of knowledge." The learner plays the "receiver of
  wisdom," passively accepting the intelligence being dispersed, like
  an empty bowl into which water is poured.[18]

In spite of this lack of consensus regarding the teaching-learning process
itself, the teacher's role can be divided into *four primary tasks.* These usually occur sequentially but can also occur in a random/repeat mode:

Planning: All teaching-learning experiences require planning; the design of the curriculum depends upon the learning objectives.

Communication: Although there is more to the total process, nothing happens unless information is made available to the learner.

Guidance: The learner needs to be guided in applying and/or attempting to understand the information.

Evaluation: The achievement of the learner needs to be assessed, feedback provided, and remedial measures instituted.

It can be hypothesized that anything that allows the teacher to perform these tasks better should *enhance learning.* This premise is used as the basis for empowering teachers with technology. To elaborate:

- *Planning.* What happens in the classroom requires planning. *What* to teach, *when* to teach it, and *how* to teach it are determined by the learning objectives. Considering the press of classroom responsibilities and the teacher's lack of training regarding technology, teachers must be provided a *template* that prescribes how technology is to be deployed. Thus, the task of planning does not depend upon trial and error, the time-consuming selection of software, or retraining.

- *Communication.* Although each of the four tasks is integral to the process, the communication of information is the essence of education. Stated another way, information is the fuel that powers the teaching-learning process. Anything the teacher does to improve the *quality* of the fuel or the *fidelity* of the information, its relevance to the course objectives, and its accessibility should boost learning. Empowered with technology, teachers can readily make visually rich, course-specific multimedia available to learners in an individualized, interactive mode.

- *Guidance.* The learner needs to be guided in order to understand and/or apply the information. The teacher compensates for the disparity in individual learner aptitude by one-on-one tutoring. In the real world of classrooms, the amount of guidance provided is seldom as much as the teacher would choose. Empowered with computers programmed with course-specific software, the teacher can readily provide guidance *based on the learner's need, not the teacher's availability.*

- *Evaluation.* The achievement of the learner needs to be assessed. Ideally, feedback would be provided and remedial measures initiated on an individualized basis. In the real world of the classroom, the extent to which this is accomplished depends wholly on the size of the class and the time constraints placed upon the teacher. The Technology-Enhanced Curriculum (TEC) allows teachers to deploy computers to evaluate, provide feedback, and immediately initiate remedial measures. And, again, all of this is based on the needs of the *learner* rather than the availability of the *teacher.*

Perception

Teachers plan, communicate, guide, and evaluate. Information technology can be adapted to allow the teacher to do these better and, thus, impact positively the efficiency of the teaching-learning process.

THE PRIMACY OF THE WORD IN EDUCATION

The classroom is a world that centers on books, chalkboards, and teacher-talk. As previously noted, teaching and learning still exists as a word-oriented process at a time when, beyond the classroom walls, our youth thrive in an electronically generated, visually rich environment.

Perception

For centuries, the teaching-learning process has been primarily fueled by words—the lecture and the book—mainly because until now teachers have always found words easier to use; not because it was determined that words impact learners better than the combination of words and images.

To put this matter into perspective, consider the following: when early humans decided to store information in order to communicate with the future, they instinctively used *pictures.* And so, on the walls of tombs and temples, in primeval caves, and in dark catacombs, the ancients chiseled and painted images.

Then, as civilization developed, humans realized the need to record and transmit feelings, ideas, concepts, and other intangible information. When pictures became inadequate, the Phoenicians in the eleventh century devised a system to replicate the spoken word—the alphabet. Although specialized skills were required, literacy was easier to acquire than the skill to produce etchings in stone. Those empowered with literacy represented the power structure of that day. They were the scholars and the kingpins of an emerging primary societal institution—education.

Progressing in time, it came to pass that the heart of the medieval classroom was the exalted font of human knowledge—on a pedestal at the front of the room—the book. Since it was tediously produced by hand, there were few books and they were indeed exalted. Thus, the *primacy of the word* was born in education: the book and the lecture—a remarkably endurable tradition.

In 1450, Gutenberg gave birth to his brainchild, the printing press, and the world was never the same. The book fueled the rebirth of mankind—the Renaissance. From then until now, universal literacy became the norm for all civilized countries, and the tempo of societal change markedly accelerated. Literally thousands of traditions have come and gone since 1450, but one tradition endures: the book still remains ingrained as the core of the culture of learning—coexisting with the lecture and later the chalkboard. Incredibly, the *primacy of the word* in education has survived the Industrial Age, the Technological Age, and the Information Age—alive and well.

MORE ABOUT THE CRITICAL MATTER OF PICTURES VERSUS WORDS

It is a shibboleth—and it has been around for a long time: "A picture is worth a thousand words . . ."

The logic seems irrefutable; yet, it implies that a thousand words can be substituted for a picture. How many words would it take to describe a sunset? Or the look on Jacqueline Kennedy's face on that fateful day in November 1963 as she watched Lyndon Johnson take the oath of office, succeeding her slain husband as president of the United States? A thousand words do not begin to describe all there is to communicate within these images. The time has come to put a sharper edge to that age-old adage, which perhaps understates reality.

Perception

*A verbal description alone of anything that can be seen must be con-
sidered a compromise; a compromise made every day in classrooms in
an age when technology makes it unnecessary.*

Obviously, learners cannot be brought to the 1969 moon landing as it
happened. It is necessary, therefore, to create a *replica* or a substitute
for the sensory experience of actually being there, which would be
termed the *referent*. Even if the replica were a verbal description alone
from the astronaut who actually took the first step, it must be considered
a compromise—regardless of his verbalization skills. The best replica
possible of the moon landing would be a video of the event, accompa-
nied by narration. Is there any doubt that there would be a greater impact on learners from the video than from a verbal description *alone?*
Given the choice, how many in the world would have chosen radio over
television to experience the historic event in 1969?

Thompson noted that pictures or graphics are specific, thus lacking
the sensory ambiguity that words can create.[19] Further, a verbal description—or verbal replica—of anything that can be seen represents a
particular individual's interpretation of the referent, and it is susceptible
to whatever bias or understanding that person may have. Therefore, it is
undeniably *a compromise*. Again, this compromise occurs in classrooms
all over the world, every day in an age when technology makes it unnecessary.

Another perspective: the gap between the referent and the replica, regardless of the medium used, determines what can be termed the *fidelity
of the information*. In the classroom, the greater the fidelity—or stated
another way—the greater the quality of the information, the greater the
sensory impact on the whole brain—right and left—inevitably resulting
in *more effective learning*.

One final thought on this critical matter: in presenting evidence in a
courtroom, would a verbal description, rather than an image, be made
available of anything that can be seen? Apparently, in that situation
there is *no tolerance* for compromise. Yet, for centuries, an educational
system has been in place that is primarily word-oriented. In the Digital
Age, technology can empower teachers and make this compromise unnecessary.

THE SCIENTIST'S VIEW

A matter approached in chapter 2 needs to be revisited: central to the critical matter of pictures versus words is the basic analysis of how the brain processes information. A major scientific breakthrough is the clearly established and compelling fact that humans have *two separate* information-processing systems. One is located in the left brain and deals exclusively with information in the form of sounds and digits. It is called the "auditory–digital" system. The other is located in the right brain and deals exclusively with information in the form of pictures and graphics. It is called the "visual–iconic" system.

Cassidy has reminded us that our books, chalkboard, and teacher-talk educational system is geared toward the auditory–digital left brain.[20] He concludes that our schools are ignoring half of the brain. Yet, as noted several times, outside the classroom young people live in a world rich in visual sensory stimulation—or visual–iconic inputs. *Indeed, there is a gap between the two worlds—with major adverse implications for learning.*

Houston has offered some enlightening observations.[21] She contends that before going to school, from infancy, children learn to think and to function from a much larger sensory and neurological base. They develop by relying on what they see, hear, feel, taste, and smell. In the classroom, the great bulk of the sensory inputs are to the left brain. Our educational system and our understanding of intelligence discriminates against one entire half of the brain. Thus, it tends to reward only left-hemispheric-dominant learners who respond well to verbal linear styles of education. Her most disconcerting observation: "So much of the behavioral problems and failures in school come directly out of boredom which itself comes directly out of the larger failure to stimulate all those areas in children's brains that could give them so many more ways of responding to their world."

The work of these two scientists and others provides crucial evidence regarding the critical matter of *pictures versus words* and its impact on *how* humans learn. Incredibly, it has been virtually ignored in the mainstream of educational thinking. Further, the reality is that today's user-friendly, relatively inexpensive technology makes it feasible for teachers to create, routinely, in the classroom—as in the home—visually rich, whole-brain-specific experiences. It would follow that by so doing, they would be addressing one of the root causes of why—in spite of long-term, costly efforts—we have failed to realize broad-scaled, quantifiable improvement in learner achievement.

Perception

There is compelling evidence that learning is heightened when teachers create visually rich experiences, thus engaging the learner's entire brain—rather than only half.

WHAT TEACHERS DO MOST

As already noted, teachers manage information. Although there is much more to their role, the essence of what teachers do is to make information available to learners and assist them in mentally assimilating that information.

Perception

In great part, the effectiveness of the communication phase of the teaching-learning process determines the outcome. Additionally, there are three critical factors that determine how well learners assimilate the information made available: fidelity, relevancy, and accessibility.

- *Fidelity.* Is it real or is it a replica? If it is a replica, how close is it to the real thing—the referent? Example: Did the teacher place a live rattlesnake on her desk rather than a replica? Did she show a video, project a still picture on a screen, draw a rattlesnake on the chalkboard, give a verbal description? Each of these represents a different level of *fidelity,* and, expectedly, has a different impact on learners.
- *Relevancy.* Each individual in the class has a different information bank, learning aptitude, and motivation. Is the information provided what that particular learner *needs,* what that learner *understands,* what that learner *wants*? The relevancy factor is highest in one-on-one tutoring. It is lowest in a first-year college English class of 100.

- *Accessibility.* Is the information available *when* the learner wants it, *where* the learner wants it, or as *many times* as that particular learner needs it? A book offers the highest level of accessibility, but the fidelity factor is very low since it does not store information involving motion and sound.

The value of defining these factors is that they provide criteria for determining the effectiveness of the various information-delivery approaches used by teachers and the capacity of technology to enhance that effectiveness.

EMPOWERING TEACHERS AND LEARNERS

In determining how the teacher's capacity to make information available to learners can be progressively improved, the matter of empowering teachers is analyzed in context with the *fidelity, relevancy,* and *accessibility* factors:

1. *Start with the teacher talking to a class without an aid of any kind.* The *fidelity* of the information depends solely on the teacher's ability to provide verbal descriptions and the learner's capacity to perceive them. The *relevancy* to each learner depends—in great part—on his or her individual capability and the amount of interaction with the teacher. The *accessibility* for future study depends on the completeness and accuracy of the learner's note taking—if notes are taken.
2. *Now empower the teacher with a chalkboard.* The *fidelity* is improved, depending on the teacher's ability to draw. Interaction is somewhat improved by eliciting and then listing key points, words, and so forth. The quality of the learner's notes is improved by being able to copy from the chalkboard.
3. *Empower teachers with a support system to provide the learner printed materials.* Printed images decrease the compromise of verbal descriptions and, thus, increase *fidelity.* Books, manuals, and handouts allow self-study. To some degree, learners can answer their own questions to improve *relevancy.* Learners can

also retrieve information at their own pace, and *accessibility* increases.

4. *Empower the teacher with an overhead or slide projector.* The teacher can now narrate over images; *fidelity* is improved. Listing the main points on a transparency and using graphics facilitate interaction and increase *relevancy.* They provide the teacher access, while lecturing, to information beyond what can be stored in and retrieved from the teacher's memory. Since transparencies are stored by the teacher, *accessibility* to this information by the learner is limited.

5. *Empower the teacher with the use of video with no learner self-retrieval mode.* This represents a marked increase in *fidelity.* In addition to images in motion, it is possible to provide sounds. It represents the best possible replica and eliminates the compromise of using verbal descriptions of what can be seen. Limitation: the information is not accessible to the learner for self-study.

6. *Provide the learner access to the video in a self-retrieval mode.* The *fidelity* factor remains the same. However, it is obvious that the *accessibility* factor is markedly increased. There is also some improvement in the relevancy in that the learner can fast-forward and skip some segments and rewind and review other segments as many times as needed.

7. *Provide the learner access to a computer programmed with course-specific software.* This introduces a new and powerful dimension to the process—*interactivity.* The computer can be programmed to function as a tutor, addressing those parts of the lesson required for review by an individual learner. Now, all three factors—*fidelity, relevancy,* and *accessibility*—can be considered optimal.

8. *Provide learners access to the Internet.* By integrating the search for information on the Internet into the curriculum, the teacher can vastly expand the amount of information accessible to the learner, its *relevancy,* and its *accessibility.* "Information overload" is a major limitation. This additional dimension to the process is more productive at the higher educational levels as learners become more adept at using the Internet and managing their own learning experiences.

Perception

Information technology skillfully integrated into the curriculum will allow teachers to improve the fidelity, relevancy, and accessibility of the information they make available to learners. It is proposed that this empowers teachers so that they might do what they do—better.

A REVIEW OF PERCEPTIONS

The perceptions offered in this chapter are intended to share some basic insights regarding technology's role in the classroom. To review:

- Human progress from the Stone Age to the Information Age resulted primarily from amplifying individuals' capacity to function, first by empowering them with crude implements, then tools, then machines, and now technology. This is basic to understanding how teachers can do what they do—*better.*
- All human activity is driven by information; the more demanding the activity—the greater the need for information. Thus, information can be termed the *fuel* that powers the teaching-learning process.
- At a fundamental level, it can be assumed that all learning is initiated by information perceived by the senses: specifically, what you see, hear, taste, smell, and feel.
- Information technology empowers teachers by amplifying their capacity to readily provide their learners the *heightened* sensory perceptions of multimedia.
- The master teachers of the Information Age are those who develop the capacity to navigate the worldwide oceans of information and selectively retrieve that which can provide an enriched experience for their learners.
- How teachers manage information has a major impact on the *outcome* of the teaching-learning process. Technology facilitates and amplifies the teacher's capacity to provide learners with information of *higher fidelity* in an individualized, interactive mode.
- Teachers *plan, communicate, guide,* and *evaluate.* Information technology can be adapted to allow the teacher to do these better

and, thus, impact positively the efficiency of the teaching-learning process.

- For centuries, the teaching-learning process has been primarily fueled by words—the lecture and the book—mainly because until now teachers have always found words easier to use; not because it was determined that *words impact learners better than the combination of words and images.*

- A verbal description alone of anything that can be seen must be considered a compromise; a compromise made every day in classrooms in an age when technology makes it *unnecessary.*

- There is compelling evidence that learning is heightened when teachers create visually rich experiences, thus engaging the learner's entire brain—rather than *only half.*

- In great part, the effectiveness of the communication phase of the teaching-learning process determines the outcome.

- Information technology skillfully integrated into the curriculum will allow teachers to improve the fidelity, relevancy, and accessibility of the information they make available to learners. It is proposed that this empowers teachers so that they might do what they do—*better.*

ONE FINAL THOUGHT

The next two chapters provide an overview of what have come to be considered the *core* information technologies—television and computers. Understanding how they manage information is basic to understanding the two new models of education to be introduced later. Additionally, understanding why their potential to amplify the teacher's capacity to function has not as yet been realized is basic to understanding the strategies to be proposed.

NOTES

1. Tyler, Keith I. and Williams, Catherine M., *Educational Communication in a Revolutionary Age.* Worthington, OH: Jones Publishing, 1973, p. 2.

2. Dierker, Robert, "The Future of Electronic Education," in *The Electronic Classroom: A Handbook for Education in the Electronic Environment,* ed. Erwin Boschman. Medford, NJ: Learned Information, 1995, p. 228.

3. Asimov, Isaac, "Our Race with Doom," *TV Guide.* Vol. 19, No. 23, June 5, 1971, p. 5.

4. Thompson James, J., *Instructional Communication.* New York: American Book Company, 1969, p. 199.

5. Houston, Jean, "Education and Its Transformations," in *Education: A Time for Decisions,* ed. Kathleen M. Redd and Arthur M. Harkins. Washington, DC: World Future Society, 1980, p. 145.

6. Thornburg, David, D., *Education in the Communication Age.* San Carlos, CA: Thornburg and Starsong, 1994, p. 35.

7. Perelman, Lewis J., *School's Out.* New York: Avon, 1992, p. 28.

8. Heldman, Robert K., *Future Telecommunications.* New York: McGraw-Hill, 1993, p. 40.

9. Perelman, *School's Out,* p. 30.

10. Perelman, *School's Out,* p. 30.

11. Perelman, *School's Out,* p. 35.

12. Gentry, Cass G., "Educational Technology in the 1990s," in *Instructional Technology: Past, Present, and Future,* ed. Gary Anglin. Englewood, CO: Libraries Unlimited, 1991, p. 27.

13. Stoll, Clifford, *Silicon Snake Oil: Second Thoughts on the Information Highway.* New York: Doubleday, 1995, p. 3.

14. Thompson, James J., *Instructional Technology.* New York: American Book Company, 1969, p. 199.

15. Percival, M. and Ellington, R., *A Handbook of Educational Technology.* New York: Nichols, 1984, p. 40.

16. Gagne, Robert M., "Foundations in Learning Research," in *Instructional Technology: Foundations,* ed. Robert Gagne. Hillside, NJ: Lawrence Erlbaum, 1987, p. 49.

17. Fuhrman, B., and A. Grasha, *Practical Handbook for the College Teachers.* Boston: Little, Brown, and Co, 1983, p. 60.

18. Perelman, *School's Out,* p. 261.

19. Thompson, *Instructional Technology,* p. 4.

20. Cassidy, Michael F., "Visual Literacy: A Failed Metaphor," *ECTJ.* Vol. 31, No. 2, 1983, p. 67.

21. Houston, "Education and Its Transformations," p. 149.

5

EDUCATIONAL TELEVISION: A 50-YEAR PERSPECTIVE

Television's immediacy creates a compelling personal experience.

—Michael T. Romano

About this chapter:

- It is structured around a series of interrelated perceptions.
- It provides a 50-year perspective of educational television.
- It suggests that understanding the "ETV story" will be useful in the current effort to empower teachers with computers and the Internet.
- It reviews the circumstances that fostered the early union of television and education.
- It underscores television's profound impact on society, first nationally and then globally.
- It notes the early optimism regarding television's potential to enhance what happens in the classroom.
- It defines television's potential role in amplifying the teacher's capacity to function.
- It analyzes the flaws in the utilization strategy responsible for the failure to realize the expectations.

WHY REVISIT EDUCATIONAL TELEVISION?

It was the 1950s and I was there. The expectations were enormous and the excitement was high. As a young educator, I joined the ranks of the enthusiasts who believed *the future was now.* I became a bona fide techno-geek of that day.

Television had established itself as an engaging, new presence in the living room, and its impact was profound. The challenge was clear: adapt this powerful, compelling medium to help cultivate young minds in the classroom. But, incredibly, it simply did not happen.

In 1988, Cohen expressed the views of many when he wrote: "Many innovations have swept across the nation's schools, generally finding hundreds of applications, but inevitably disappearing quietly leaving few traces of their existence. Thus, it has been for educational television."[1]

This chapter provides an analysis of what went wrong with ETV so that, hopefully, the mistakes will not be repeated with computers and the Internet.

STARTING AT THE BEGINNING

Now, after almost 50 years, it can be told. To some, it was indeed *a marriage of convenience.* The groom had no past and came from the other side of the tracks—the world of buffoons who specialized in pie-in-the-face antics, wrestlers, prizefighters, horse-opera characters, and gum-shoe detectives.

The bride came from one of the most honored, age-old institutions of society. But she was in trouble. There was a huge surge in demand for higher education after World War II as a result of the GI Bill, which provided free tuition to veterans. It is to the credit of a few visionaries in education who, early on, instinctively believed that television had the capacity to serve as an expediency in dealing with a growing teacher shortage.

To the visionaries, the rationale was obvious. If it could place Milton Berle in millions of living rooms and create a mind-grabbing experience, why couldn't it place a good teacher in more than one classroom? Perhaps even in living rooms? All that was necessary—the visionaries insisted—was money, effort, and the desire to make it work. It had to be a *good marriage*.

Indeed, over the subsequent decades, tons of money were expended, and many worked tirelessly—but it would become painfully obvious that the desire on the part of most in education was lacking. Teachers instinctively felt, from the beginning, that if television really could teach, their professional security would be compromised—*an understandably disquieting possibility*.

Then it was 1957, and following several years of effort at major university centers throughout the country, the time came to sit down and talk. The credentials of those who participated in this first national conference on the use of television in education were indeed impressive. The conference was hosted by Pennsylvania State University and was sponsored by the Ford Foundation, the Fund for the Advancement of Education, and the American Council on Education. It was a remarkable effort to make the marriage respectable. Indeed, the commitment to the marriage was real.

In the preface to the report on the conference, published in 1958, C. R. Carpenter, director of Academic Research and Services, Pennsylvania State University, wrote:

> Plans for this conference are based on the premises that: (1) television as an instrument of education has earned an established role in American education; (2) television's place in education needs to be greatly expanded and its effectiveness improved; and (3) the most crucial and promising possibilities lie in improving the processes of teaching and learning by television.[2]

Most of the speakers at the conference described what was being done with television at institutions around the country to explore the apparently rich potential of the master medium to further the mission of education. Undoubtedly, the black box with the magic glass face.would join the book and the chalkboard as a significant, new, permanent accoutrement of the classroom.

Carpenter reports that in the midst of properly restrained enthusiasm one professor sounded a sobering note. His paper was entitled, "I Think TV Teaching Is a Good Idea, But—." Cautiously, and yet deliberately, he shared his observation that in actuality many teachers felt somewhat threatened by television. That, in essence, the use of television in the classroom represented a new, unfamiliar practice against the background of old, traditional ways. "There exists," he stated, "the explicit *fear* that television is capable of decreasing the need for teachers."[3]

This negative mind-set was indeed more deeply rooted than initially realized. It has persisted for almost 50 years. In retrospect, it is in great part responsible for the failure to realize fully the remarkable, rich potential of television as a versatile servant of education; a medium that *skillfully* adapted is capable of enhancing the teacher's capacity to deliver vastly improved, visually rich information to learners. A medium with the potential to *enhance* the teacher's status rather than *compromise* it.

THE TELEVISION REVOLUTION: IMPACT ON SOCIETY

Before focusing closely on the marriage of television and education, it should be helpful to briefly review the broader implications of this remarkable electronic master medium.

Commercial television has emerged as a multibillion-dollar global enterprise whose impact on the human condition has been—by any standard—enormous. Essentially, it is a "window to the world." In other words, television represents nothing less than the global extension of the human sensorium, allowing the individual to feel connected, thus *providing a unique, compelling, personal experience.* As Thompson aptly states, "Television's immediate transmission of sight and sound— probably the two most important modes of human communication— interlaces the world, inciting change that is at once swift, profound and often disorienting."[4]

This much is certain: television is relevant, it is riveting, and it provides the human psyche with daily doses of everything that is beautiful and everything that is ugly in our universe. What is disconcerting is that by the age of 18 years, most American youth have spent 15,000 hours in front of a television screen compared with 11,000 hours in front of a teacher in a classroom.[5] Most significantly, television provides sensory stimulation for the *whole brain*. The teacher, with only books and chalkboard—for the most part—stimulates *only half*.

Perception

Television empowers individuals by amplifying their capacity to see and hear virtually anything, anywhere. Essentially, it is an extension of the human sensorium, and its immediacy makes it authentic, unique, compelling, and powerful. Outside the classroom, children absorb it for hours, appearing to develop a virtual dependency *on the whole-brain sensory perceptions it provides.*

This is the phenomenon—the television revolution. It is spawning global markets, fueling the global economy, and amalgamating global society.

THE ETV STORY CONTINUES

The early proponents of educational television shared the common vision that a qualified teacher brought before a class by television was *more effective* than an unqualified teacher in person. It was this premise that served as the basis for the National Defense Education Act of 1952 that for 20 years provided funds for linking the country with a series of statewide educational television networks.[6]

The costly effort to blanket the nation with ETV had the following clearly defined goals incorporated in the legislation: address the serious teacher shortage, overcome the unequal distribution of educational resources, and provide additional educational opportunities for adults.

The claim then was that the development of educational television networks provided an efficient, effective means of delivering instruction into classrooms and homes. In an effort to secure funding, proponents emphasized its cost advantage: quality instruction, some enthusiasts insisted, could be delivered literally at a per-child cost of a pencil. This sounded great to everyone except, understandably, *teachers*. Many perceived it as a *threat* that placed their livelihoods at risk. Indeed, this was a legitimate concern.

In spite of this, a bandwagon phenomenon occurred. The first ETV network was developed in Texas in 1953. By 1970, more than half the states were on board. Regrettably, a good-faith assessment of the number of teachers willing to ride along was never made. Later, it became evident that this was a critical mistake, as it became clear that grassroots support for the new miracle medium was lacking. In reality, what existed were *islands of enthusiasm in a vast sea of apathy and anxiety*.

THE POTENTIAL OF TELEVISION IN EDUCATION

The literature is replete with evidence that the medium can do many things—and it can do some things *exceedingly well*. In an effort to determine the status of educational television, in 1967 the U.S. Office of Education commissioned a study of the research on educational television in the United States.[7] The final report noted there were 269 projects reported in the literature between 1957 and 1967. Essentially, the applications of television in education reported by 1967, and those attempted subsequently, can be categorized as follows:

- Replicating teachers and televising them to several small sections of a large-enrollment college course. This is done with or without teaching assistants at section sites.
- Replicating master teachers and televising them to classes in school districts where qualified teachers in certain subjects are not available.
- Replicating courses and televising them to homes, allowing professionals to participate in continuing-education experiences. This approach has been used for college credit and high school equivalency diploma programs.
- Delivering in-service training to groups of teachers and administrators throughout a school district.
- Providing the capacity for image magnification to enhance and facilitate in-class demonstrations of all kinds.
- Providing supplemental/enrichment motion picture materials, delivered by video. A teacher-operated videocassette or DVD system are markedly more convenient than the classroom use of a motion picture projection setup.

- Making feasible self-confrontation-by-videotape techniques for teaching skills of all kinds. The learner's performance is recorded and then the tape is reviewed with or without the teacher.

HOW TELEVISION EMPOWERS TEACHERS

In addition to the applications listed, the unique potential of television in education must be viewed in terms of what it can do to amplify the capacity of the classroom teacher to manage audible and visible information. The matter of words versus pictures was discussed in detail in chapter 4. As noted, television can empower teachers with the capacity to enhance the fidelity, relevancy, and accessibility of the information they are making available to learners, which, it can be assumed, impacts favorably on the outcome. To elaborate:

- *Fidelity*. If it can be seen and/or heard, it can be replicated by television with high fidelity and made available to the learner. The compromise of using verbal descriptions of anything that can be seen is eliminated, and the teaching-learning process is fueled by visually rich information of higher fidelity and, therefore, is enhanced.
- *Relevancy*. Video created *specifically* for a curriculum makes the visually rich information imparted by the teacher relevant, cogent, and compelling. Theoretically, the right brain and left brain are stimulated equally to the benefit of the learner. Thus, the gap between the world of the classroom and the world beyond its walls is bridged.
- *Accessibility*. Videocassette and DVD technology facilitates the retrieval of stored audible and visible information and makes it accessible to the learner on a group basis, under the tutelage of a teacher in the classroom, or on an individualized basis elsewhere, including the home.

Perception

Television empowers teachers by amplifying their capacity to improve the efficacy of the information fueling the teaching-learning process;

specifically, by enhancing the fidelity, relevancy, and accessibility of the information made available to learners. This potential has not been fully realized in great part because it has generally not been understood.

Within the next decade, it can be speculated that the use of television and computer technology in education will converge. All audible and visible information will be stored and retrieved in a digital/interactive mode on an individual or group-presentation basis. Although the technology is presently available, it most likely will not become the standard in education until *all teachers* are computer-literate and there is a support system in place to produce *curriculum-specific software*.

TELEVISION AND EDUCATION: THE STATE OF THE UNION

It isn't talked about openly, but the *marriage of convenience* has not worked as well as the original sponsors had hoped. Although the union of television and education has survived almost 50 years, there are unrealized expectations and keen frustration for the early visionaries and enthusiasts.

At a point, the ETV networks faced certain hard facts. Yes, the original expectations of using television to decrease the need for teachers and to equalize the quality of instruction are entirely feasible. This is confirmed by literally tons of research. No, it became evident, these particular goals are not generally attainable in the existing system of education.

Additionally, the National Defense Education Act of 1952 funded the construction of ETV networks so that the general public would avail itself of educational experiences. In reality, great numbers of people opted to watch the pie-in-the-face buffoons on commercial television rather than a talking head discussing Alexander the Great. These were the incontrovertible facts faced by the nation's ETV networks in the late 1960s.

Thus, as does any entity faced with decline, educational television went into *survival mode*. Unobtrusively, the original, primary mission of televising teachers in classrooms was scaled down and modified. Then, the networks turned their attention to emphasizing and improving what was initially intended as a secondary mission—serving the general public.

FROM ETV TO PBS

In 1968, the Corporation for Public Broadcasting (CPB) was formed, and a year later educational television networks joined CPB to create a consortium called the Public Broadcasting Service (PBS). The viewing public was given an alternative to commercial television, called public television, which was promoted as *enrichment television*.

From the beginning, programming was excellent. Early on, the talking heads were replaced by rich, visual depictions of history, nature, science, drama, and whatever else the world had to offer. Soon, a loyal audience of public television aficionados evolved. Initially, the CPB derived most of its funding from the federal government. In recent years, money from private sources has replaced lost federal funds.

This scenario—the quiet mutation of the educational television networks into public television—played out over several years and essentially tells the story of education and its grandiose expectations for the master medium—television. In 1991, Cambre wrote what some considered an epitaph for educational television. She noted that, insofar as the classroom is concerned several scholars prominent in the field of educational technology have written it off as a *failed* medium.[8]

ETV: THE EXPECTATIONS GAP

Actually, today a great deal of important work is being done with television in our schools and in extending educational opportunities beyond its walls. However, educational television is a *failure* in terms of the original, primary mission; specifically, to *improve the quality of education, particularly in economically depressed areas.*

Developments in the Commonwealth of Kentucky can be cited.[9] KET, or the Kentucky Network as it is called, is the largest public television network in the United States. It was created in 1968. Then, in 1990, the state legislature passed sweeping legislation called the Kentucky Education Reform Act. One of the act's basic objectives is to address the existing inequity in the quality of education throughout the commonwealth. This can be interpreted as an indication that the mandate given the Kentucky statewide ETV network in 1968—namely, to equalize the quality of education throughout the state—was simply not realized, in spite of the valiant efforts made by many dedicated people. For the most part, these are the realities regarding ETV throughout the nation.

One additional point: the 1995 study by the U.S. Congress Office of Technology concluded that, in 1991, the typical school had seven TVs and six videocassette recorders. It reported that most teachers made some use of video presentations during the school year, but data about kinds of use and effectiveness was lacking.[10]

One thing is certain: the use of television in education over the past 50 *years* did not result in any measurable *improvement in learner achievement scores*.

APPROACHING THE CRITICAL QUESTION

There is no doubt that after years of costly trial and error, the great expectations raised in the 1950s and 1960s regarding the use of the television in the classroom have not been realized. Yet, there is a great deal that can be stated with certainty in answer to the basic question: *can television teach?*

No—it cannot teach first-graders how to interact with others, how to think, and how to learn.

Yes—it can teach a first-grader, for example, how to cross a street safely, how a tadpole becomes a frog, or what makes it rain, all without leaving the classroom.

No—it cannot teach a surgical resident how to perform brain surgery.

Yes—it can teach a surgical resident the steps in a brain surgery procedure so that his or her experience as a learner at the operating table can be more meaningful and productive.

No—it cannot teach a seventh-grader the full story of the Civil War without the aid of a teacher, a textbook, and class discussions.

Yes—it can depict and, therefore, teach a seventh-grader the horror and the intensity of the Battle of Atlanta with infinitely more impact than only a teacher, a textbook, and a chalkboard.

No—it cannot replace teachers, textbooks, and seminars in preparing a graduate student in history.

Yes—it can make a seminar—for example, on the Vietnam War—more meaningful for the graduate student by presenting Henry Kissinger on video relating his account of the talks leading to peace.

No—it cannot replace a teacher and a laboratory experience in preparing a dental technician.

Yes—it can make a laboratory session more efficient and effective by providing at the learner's workstation a self-retrievable, step-by-step video demonstration of a procedure to be mastered.

No—it cannot replace a live fully qualified high school physics teacher.

Yes—it can provide a televised qualified high school physics teacher who will be more effective than an unqualified live teacher.

No—it cannot replace teachers, textbooks, and seminars in preparing a student teacher to interact effectively with learners.

Yes—it can allow self-confrontation by videotape as an extremely effective adjunct to procedures for preparing classroom teachers.

This list can go on and on. However, the point is abundantly clear: after 50 years, there is a great deal we know—with certainty—about television's great potential as a versatile servant of education. Yet, compared with what *can* be done, it is evident that what *is being done* is minimal.

Perception

Ironically, television, the global master medium that daily impacts human psyches and emotions in homes, is only an occasional visitor in the classroom—the place where young minds are being nurtured and cultivated. This is because we have not yet devised the best way to harness this extraordinary power in a manner compatible with the system in place.

THE ETV EXPECTATIONS GAP ANALYZED

There are four primary factors responsible for the failure to realize the full potential of television in education: these are conflict with the teacher's traditional role, failure to make televised lessons completely curriculum-specific, faulty adaptation, and the perception of television as a passive medium.

I. Television versus the Teacher's Traditional Role

Thompson's views on educational television and teachers in 1969 are still valid today—a quarter of a century later:

> From the beginning, ETV seemed destined to alienate the classroom teacher. Not a "grass roots" movement in education, it was imposed on the teaching community by educational administration. They obediently switched on the television receivers at program time but were often amused and disinterested onlookers rather than active participants. Inevitably, their attitudes seemed to rub off on learners.
>
> In many instances, television was made to broadcast content and pedagogy that were themselves unsound. Television merely permitted education to see itself as others saw it and we did not like what we saw. Like book burners, we turned on the medium instead of our own inadequacies. But, good ideas cannot be burned or ridiculed away, and television is a good idea.[11]

Television is capable of breaching the traditional sanctity of the classroom and can create a "double intrusion" situation. Theoretically, television can supplant a classroom teacher with a noninteractive, televised replica. Also, it can allow others, elsewhere, to "look in" on what a classroom teacher is doing with his or her class.

Undeniably, all of this seriously compromises tradition and is anxiety-provoking for teachers. Unfortunately, this critical situation was not approached in a forthright manner early on, nor was it reconciled to the satisfaction of all parties involved. Hence, the genesis of some teachers' understandably negative attitude toward the use of television.

It should be noted that 40 years ago the proponents of educational television were cautioned that teachers would resist any attempt to usurp—to any extent—their traditional central role in the classroom.[12] Still, in 1995 an official of a major national higher-education organization—ignoring reality—wrote: "We are still experimenting and learning which topics, modes of presentation, distribution and pricing make the most attractive alternatives to live sessions."[13]

Perception

Experience over the past 50 years indicates that any application of television—or any technology—that compromises the teacher's traditional role in the classroom inevitably will engender resistance.

Inevitably, any strategy intended to make the *elusive connection* between teachers, learners, and technology must come to terms with this fact of academic life. The model of education to be introduced later in this book empowers teachers and amplifies their capacity rather than compromising their role in any way.

2. The Curriculum-Specific Challenge

Traditionally, teachers create their own curricula based on predetermined objectives. This involves not only *what* to teach but *when* to teach it. Televising lessons simultaneously into multiple classrooms that articulate into the myriad of existing curricula is a formidable challenge—a challenge that has not been addressed successfully, thus impeding the acceptance of ETV.

In the late 1970s, low-cost video recorders made the scene. Allowing schools to record the televised lessons made it feasible to better integrate these into the curriculum schedule in place. However, dealing with this one factor was not enough to overcome the other barriers to realizing the full potential of ETV.

3. Faulty Adaptation

Obviously, television can be adapted to a host of applications, and the degree of adaptation determines the effectiveness. This "concept of adaptation" has not been generally understood regarding the use of television in education.[14] Often, the result has been a mismatch similar to having a farmer use a jetliner to spray a cotton field. To elaborate:

Initially, all educational television was created in the image of commercial television. In many instructional applications, superimposing the high-tech world of broadcast TV on academe was unnecessary and severely compromised the end result. The teacher was intimidated, frustrated, anxious, and disenchanted; just as the farmer would be if the only way to apply chemicals to crops was to use a jet airliner. This erroneous mind-set regarding television utilization techniques *still endures*.

In education, television, like print, can be utilized in a wide variety of production levels. At the low end, for instance, we use print extemporaneously when taking lecture notes or writing on a chalkboard. Then, there are photocopied class handouts and soft-covered manuals. Finally, there is the high-end production level—textbooks. This same phenomenon of *variable production levels* applies to the use of television in education. Image magnification in a biology laboratory requires a vastly different, less demanding approach than producing a biology unit for utilization on the state ETV network. This simple reality was not generally understood and the results were counterproductive.

Thompson said it best: "We have seen—and this cannot be overemphasized—that instructional television needs to develop *a format of its own* rather than imitate commercial television, the traditional classroom or the teaching laboratory."[15] Later in this book, such a format will be introduced.

Perception

Television's primary role in education is not to supplant teachers. Rather, it can be adapted to supplement their capacity to impart audible and visible information, thus enhancing the fuel that powers the teaching-learning process and consequently the outcome.

4. Perceiving Television as a Passive Medium

Educational television has been dismissed by many on the basis that it tends to be a passive medium. It should be noted that the textbook is also passive, but it has maintained its eminent status in education for many centuries. Television is passive only when effort and imagination have not been expended to make it an *active, exciting, compelling* medium for imparting audible and visible information to learners.

> *Passive*. A teacher presses the play button on a VCR and sits in the back of the room while learners view a videotape from start to finish with no interruption.
>
> *Active*. A teacher stands next to a TV monitor, remote control in hand. At selected intervals, the teacher stops the videotape and engages

the learners in a discussion regarding content. The chalkboard might be used as it is traditionally to embellish the interaction. Then, back to the tape.

Passive. A teacher in a physics laboratory shows a videotape of the experiment to be performed by the learners.

Active. A teacher in a physics laboratory, empowered with a simple TV image-magnification system, performs the experiment and involves the learners in discussion at each step of the procedure. Or, as a follow-up to the reading assignment in the laboratory manual, the teacher invites a learner to come up front, sit at the TV demonstration table, and perform the experiment.

Passive. A learner in the process of mastering a skill watches a videotape of someone else's performance.

Active. A learner in the process of mastering a skill is videotaped by the teacher empowered with a camcorder. The teacher—remote control in hand—stands next to the TV monitor and plays the tape. Then, a discussion ensues as the class critiques the learner's performance.

Passive. Learners in an English literature class read a play by Shakespeare. Then, they watch a videotaped performance of the work while the teacher sits in the back of the room.

Active. Learners read a play by Shakespeare. Then—remote control in hand—the teacher stands next to the TV monitor and plays the tape. At selected intervals, the teacher stops the tape and engages the class in discussion. Then, back to the tape.

Perception

The use of television in education can be either a passive or an active experience for learners. The outcome depends solely upon the teacher's understanding of television's versatility.

THE FUTURE OF TELEVISION AND EDUCATION: GIVING IT A NEW LIFE

The rationale for linking television to teaching and learning is based on the human's intolerance to accepting compromises—when an alternative is available. It has been noted earlier that *a verbal description alone of anything that can be seen must be considered a compromise.* Television has the potential to help teachers eliminate this compromise and thereby enhance the teaching-learning process.

At the annual meeting of the Society for the Advancement of Learning Technology in 1996, the keynote speaker made this plea: "We need to *revisit* the use of television in education. When we do, I feel certain we will give it *a new life.*"

The *Technology-Enhanced Curriculum* model introduced in this book unites television and education in a *new union* that will be entirely compatible with what teachers traditionally do. The format is termed *Teacher-Narrated Video* and it is described subsequently.

Perception

Television's fundamental role in the classroom is to allow teachers to eliminate the compromise of using verbal descriptions of anything that can be seen, thus enhancing the quality of the information they make available to learners, enhancing the outcome of the teaching-learning process.

A REVIEW OF PERCEPTIONS

In this chapter an understanding of television and its role in education has been approached by offering a series of reality-based, interrelated conclusions:

Television empowers individuals by amplifying their capacity to see and hear virtually anything, anywhere. Essentially, it is an extension of the human sensorium, and its immediacy makes it authentic, unique, compelling, and powerful. Outside the classroom, children absorb it for hours, appearing to develop a *virtual dependency* on the whole-brain sensory perceptions it provides.

Television empowers teachers by amplifying their capacity to improve the efficacy of the information fueling the teaching-learning process; specifically, by enhancing the fidelity, relevancy, and accessibility of the information made available to learners. This potential has not been fully realized, in great part, because it has generally not been *understood*.

Ironically, television, the global master medium that daily impacts on human psyches and emotions in homes, is only an occasional visitor in the classroom—the place where young minds are being nurtured and cultivated. This is because we have not yet devised the best way to harness this extraordinary power in a manner *compatible* with the system in place.

Experience over the past 50 years indicates that any application of television—or any technology—that compromises the teacher's traditional role in the classroom inevitably will *engender resistance*.

Television's primary role in education is not to supplant teachers. Rather, it can be adapted to supplement their capacity to impart audible and visible information, thus *enhancing the fuel that powers the teaching-learning process and consequently the outcome*.

The use of television in education can be either a passive or an active experience for learners. The outcome depends solely upon the teacher's understanding of television's *versatility*.

Television's fundamental role in the classroom is to allow teachers to eliminate the compromise of using verbal descriptions of anything that can be seen, thus enhancing the quality of the information they make available to learners, enhancing the outcome of the teaching-learning process.

ONE FINAL THOUGHT

The concept of Teacher-Narrated Video to be introduced later portends that eventually the marriage of television and education will be acknowledged on a par with other great, irrefutably successful unions, such as television and sports, television and news, television and politics, television and religion, television and entertainment, television and advertising, television and . . . *is there a need to go further?*

NOTES

1. Cohen, David H., *Technology in Education: Looking toward 2020.* Hillsdale, NJ: Lawrence Erlbaum, 1988, p. 253.

2. Carpenter, C. R., preface, in *College Teaching by Television,* by C. Adams, C. R. Carpenter, and D. R. Smith. Washington, DC: American Council on Education, 1958, p. 74.

3. Adams, C., Carpenter, C. R., and Smith, D. R., *College Teaching by Television.* Washington, DC: American Council on Education, 1958, p. 92.

4. Thompson, James J., *Instructional Communication.* New York: American Book Company, 1969, p. 107.

5. Minow, Newton N., *Abandoned in the Wasteland: Children, Television, and the First Amendment.* New York: Hill and Chang, 1995, p. 237.

6. Nugent, Given C., "Innovations in Telecommunications," in *Instructional Technology: Foundations,* ed. Robert Gagne. Hillsdale, NJ: Lawrence Erlbaum, 1987, p. 262.

7. Clu, G. C. and Schramm, W., *Learning from Television: What the Research Says.* Washington, DC: National Association of Educational Broadcasters, 1967, p. 43.

8. Cambre, Marjorie A., "The State of the Art of Instructional Television," in *Instructional Technology: Past, Present, and Future,* ed. Gary Anglin. Englewood, CO: Libraries Unlimited, 1991, p. 267.

9. University of Kentucky, Institute on Education Reform, *The Implementation of the Kentucky Technology System.* Frankfort: Kentucky Institute for Education Research, 1995, p. x.

10. U.S. Congress, Office of Technology Assessment, *Teachers and Technology: Making the Connection.* OTA-EHR-616. Washington, DC: U.S. Government Printing Office, 1995, p. 67.

11. Thompson, *Instructional Communication,* p. 115.

12. Adams, Carpenter, and Smith, *College Teaching,* p. 40.

13. Gilbert, Steven W., "Making the Most of a Slow Revolution," *Change.* March/April 1996, p. 17.

14. Romano, Michael T., "Health Science Education in the Space Age," *Annals of the New York Academy of Sciences.* Vol. 142, No. 2, March 1967, p. 348.

15. Thompson, *Instructional Communication,* p. 116.

COMPUTERS AND EDUCATION: THE ELUSIVE CONNECTION

Humans will become increasingly dependent on the mighty, minuscule microchip.

—Michael T. Romano

About this chapter:

- It reviews the computer's profound, pervasive impact on society.
- It portrays computers as amplifiers of a human's mental capacity.
- It underscores the expectations regarding computers and education.
- It defines the computer and the Internet's potential to empower teachers.
- It introduces the concept of the *new literacy* and its role in education.
- It notes the present state of the union between education and computers.
- It proposes a basic, universal application of computers in education.

THE DIGITAL AGE: A BROAD PERSPECTIVE

"The human species is about to burst the boundaries of nature and unleash the power of its technology and ingenuity, hurtling itself to the *next stage of evolution.*" This statement by Zey in 1994 has had wide reverberations in the scientific literature and the media.[1] In essence, he defined the profound implications of the so-called Digital Age.

All of this has been brought about by a development of minuscule proportions—the *mighty microchip*. One and a half million transistors can be impregnated into a silicon chip the size of a newborn infant's toenail—a cluster of microchips the size of an adult fist can provide the brainpower to guide a huge missile with a nuclear warhead from a silo on one continent to the heart of a city on another, 8,000 miles away. This is the *Digital Age*.

Then, there is the compelling phenomenon of *cyberspace*. It is an electronic entity that couples to the psyche of millions throughout the world and indulges them by interacting on a one-on-one basis. Yet, incredibly, it does not exist—as molecules. It is, in fact, *virtual reality*. It is the new frontier of the twenty-first century. It is *cyberspace*.

Ogden defined *cyberspace* as a conceptual, spaceless place where words, human relationships, data, wealth, status, and power are made manifest by people using computer-mediated communications technology.[2] It is indeed a human-made, new, significant domain—an "information superhighway" that carries the input of thousands of computers and their store of information from every country on the globe.

Like any new frontier, cyberspace presents limitless opportunity and unknown perils. Creating it was relatively simple. Dealing with the many unknowns of cyberspace is undoubtedly one of the most demanding challenges of the new millennium.

Koelsch states, "As computing and media technologies converge, the pedal will be pushed to the floor. The already rapid rate of societal change will become staggering. The *infomedia* industries—computing, communications and consumer electronics—will be the engine driving globalization."[3]

Perception

As the third millennium begins, it is evident that the development of digital technology has had, and will continue to have, a profound, pervasive impact on the course of global civilization.

BALANCING THE PERSPECTIVE: THE NEGATIVES

Inevitably, all progress exacts a toll, at the very least, living with uncertainty. The more accelerated the rate of change, the greater the toll.

Floridi, a British information scientist, reports several vexing developments that will undoubtedly challenge our collective ingenuity to its limit. He notes: "The quantity of information potentially available on the Internet has increased beyond control. Probably the most pressing issue is that we run the risk of transforming the new body of knowledge into a disjointed monster. The Internet needs a coordinated infostructure of centers that can guarantee stability and integrity of the digital encyclopedia."[4]

In 1995, Stoll received a great deal of attention in the media. This author had the audacity to buck the great digital tide engulfing society. He says, "Today's well-meaning hustlers push the Internet as universal panacea. The key ingredient of their *silicon snake oil* is a technocratic belief that computers and networks will make a *better society.*"[5]

Finally, this sobering perspective: a special issue of *Newsweek* (February 27, 1995) was entitled "TechnoMania." The lead editorial aptly summarized the phenomenon of computers and their impact on contemporary society:

> No question about it—the digital revolution is here, at last. Everything from media to medicine, from data to dating, has been radically transformed by a tool invented barely 50 years ago. The revolution has only just begun, but already it's starting to overwhelm us. It's outstripping our capacity to cope, antiquating our laws, reshuffling our economy, reordering our priorities and redefining our work places. We've aimed to separate the hope from the hype and found that in many cases the future may be very different from what the more breathless boosters of new technology now predict.

Perception

The pervasive societal developments fostered by the computer and the Internet evoke a wide disparity of reactions, since they are perceived from disparate vantage points. Regardless, all can agree on one reality: humans will become more and more dependent on the mighty, minuscule microchip. We can be optimistic that in the end, the human capacity to adapt will prevail—as it always has.

COMPUTERS AS AMPLIFIERS OF HUMAN CAPACITY

Television amplifies a human's *physical* capacity to see and hear virtually anything, anywhere. In real time, it has taken us to the depths of the ocean to view the watery grave of the *Titanic* and to the moon to witness an earthling's first step.

In the simplest terms, the computer empowers humans by amplifying their *mental* capacity. To appreciate its powerful impact on society and, more particularly, its *potential to empower teachers*, it is necessary to comprehend what computers actually do.

Perception

Computers are multimedia information-management systems that can be programmed to function on an interactive basis. They replicate and markedly amplify certain basic cognitive functions of the human mind, specifically storage, computation, and retrieval. Thus, computers have enormous potential to profoundly impact the teaching-learning process.

An elemental analysis of the cognitive functions of the mind and how they are replicated and amplified by the computer follows:

- A *human* can store and retrieve information perceived through the senses (memory). This capacity is limited, fallible, and varies from individual to individual.
- A *human empowered with a computer* infinitely amplifies the amount of information that can be stored, and its retrieval is theoretically 100 percent reliable and complete. For example,

one CD-ROM can store the equivalent of 275,000 pages of single-spaced text.

- A *human* can learn to perform a variety of complex computations. However, the capacity is limited; it is based on training and it varies depending upon the mental acuity of the individual.
- A *human empowered with a computer* can theoretically do computations of limitless complexity and do them infinitely faster and with total reliability.
- A *human* can readily interact with the mind of another human. The outcome is often unpredictable, as it depends upon a wide variety of individual variables in both parties, including the emotions.
- A *human can interact with a computer* and be assured that the response will be totally predictable and, theoretically, 100 percent reliable. This permits the design and utilization of processes and systems of superhuman complexity.

Perception

The mind coupled with a computer infinitely amplifies its capacity to perform the basic cognitive functions. Yet, there is no configuration of microchips that replicates the intricate, vital interface between mind and emotions—a basic limitation of computers.

MEMORIZATION, INTERACTION, AND ADAPTATION

To continue the elemental analysis of what computers do and their potential to enhance the teaching-learning process, consider the matter of *memory*.

Perelman reminds us that in the beginning, the storage of information was limited to what could be retained by a single brain in one lifetime. The invention of written language and then printing incrementally expanded the human capacity to store and then to share information among contemporaries and across generations.[6]

Today, a person's most accessible source of information is still the individual's own mind. Thus, memorization—the storage and retrieval of information by the mind—represents the basis for educational achievement. Evaluation—when there is no skill to be learned—is based on the retention and subsequent retrieval of information and the capacity to apply it. It can be speculated now that personal computers can free the mind of this "yoke of memorization," thereby changing the teaching-learning process markedly.

Additionally, computers have been referred to as "brain technology." Perelman suggests that we are "spinning threads that fill the world outside the human skull with growing intelligence. At the same time, what is being done holds the potential to transform the mind inside the skull as well."[7] Thus, the speculation that humans are on the verge of *a new evolutionary phase* is entirely plausible.

The critical matter of *interaction* is also a factor impacting the mind. The multimedia information stored in a computer can be retrieved on an exclusive, individualized basis. Thornburg notes that the user can craft a personal pathway through the content. He has referred to the "freedom of true interactivity" and has suggested that interactivity of this sort is rewarding at many levels. It facilitates creativity and the development of advanced thinking skills.[8]

The capacity to interact with the user is central to the computer's unique potential in education. This matter is discussed in detail subsequently.

Perception

Computers actively engage the human mind and create a synergism. However, nothing transpires unless the human takes the initiative to interact; and then the mind is locked into an active, progressive, collaborative thinking mode. Thus, in a sense, using a computer can be considered aerobics for the mind.

Finally, the concept of *adaptation* must be considered. The new and vastly amplified human capacity, through computerization, manifests itself in ways that can be mundane or mind-boggling. For instance, computers are programmed to detect impending power shortages to dwellings and to automatically bring a new source online. This computer-monitored national power grid safeguards what might be termed "society's life-support system." Computers have also allowed us to penetrate the unfathomable dimensions of outer space; to land a human on another planet and return that human safely to earth— while all the world watched.

Each of these feats required careful adaptation of basic computer technology. These adaptations—or variations—involve the creation and utilization of specialized software, the configuration of hardware, its capacity, location, and type of readout.

It is this challenge of adaptation that has not as yet been met successfully in education. *After more than 25 years of costly trial and error, there is still no specific, universally accepted basic adaptation of computers in the classroom.*

Perception

Computer technology has been adapted to amplify the capacity of professionals in virtually every aspect of society—with the exception of the teacher. Rationalizing this reality becomes increasingly difficult, since teaching and learning is an information-intensive process.

COMPUTERS AND EDUCATION: THE HYPE

In 1969, Thompson admonished teachers: "Whether you realize it or not, you have spent the last few years of your life coexisting with the computer. Now, you need to take a closer look at it. *You will be a stranger to your own students if you do not.*"[9]

The number of young people who are technically versatile has increased exponentially. In their world outside the classroom, they have literally developed a *dependency*, or what can be called a *technosymbiotic relationship*, with the TV/VCR remote, the computer mouse, and the joystick of the computer game handset. How do these young people view their teachers who—for the most part—stand before them trying to amplify their capacity to *function with a piece of chalk*?

There are voices everywhere that insist this is changing. They claim the computer is now the *new, magic, multimedia information font* of the classroom. Perhaps these are the progeny of those who in the 1950s and 1960s heralded television as the new educational miracle medium.

Cuban, a seasoned observer of the educational technology scene, comments, "The superficial similarities between periodic *gushes in enthusiasm* haunt conferences on educational technology like Marley's ghost."[10] A sample of some of the "gushes" regarding computers and education are as follows:

> 1969: Computer-assisted instruction could render much of the existing education establishment obsolete. There is a logical, sequential development of intellectual abilities that terminates when the student has mastered the content and attained the objectives of prescribed courses of study. They will save time by progressing at their own rates of comprehension. Thus, a school will be more of a process than a place.[11]
>
> 1987: The use of computer-aided delivery systems is a radical development in the history of education, representing the first qualitative change in delivery-system technology since the printing press. The computer offers something qualitatively different; that is, a way of replicating intelligent interaction with the learner. Computer-aided systems are evolving into promising alternatives to traditional delivery methods.[12]
>
> 1994: Interactive, multimedia computer systems promise to revolutionize education. The great power of these systems resides in highly sophisticated software that employs scientifically based educational methods to guide the learner through a path of instruction individually tailored to suit the special needs of each person.[13]

This kind of hype must impact negatively on those who earn their living in the classroom—teachers. Understandably, for some, the knee-jerk reaction is as it was several decades ago for educational television—*anxiety* and *more anxiety—engendering resistance*.

Everyone seems to be jumping on this latest panacea bandwagon. In the presidential campaign of 1996, President Bill Clinton and Vice President Al Gore repeatedly expressed their intention to make the Internet available to every classroom. "I want to see the day when computers are as much a part of classrooms as *chalkboards*," envisioned the president.[14]

Perception

There is a generalized intuitive feeling that computers should have a vital role in teaching and learning. What is lacking is a sharply focused definition of that role and a strategy for integrating computers into education alongside books and chalkboards—in a mode that secures the teacher's central role.

COMPUTERS AND EDUCATION: THE INTERACTIVE CAPACITY

As a beginning to understanding the potential of computers to empower teachers, consider the following.

Perception

Because computers store multimedia information interactively utilizing software that is course-specific, they allow teachers to provide each member of the class an increased number of individualized learning experiences based on the learner's needs rather than the teacher's availability.

Here are some views on interactivity (all italics added):

Schwier: "Perhaps the most salient characteristic of interactive, learning technologies is that they *engage* the learner as an active participant in the learning enterprise. Most importantly, it is a system intentionally designed to permit learners to influence the sequence, size, shape and content of the learning experience."[15]

Bunderson: "Computers allow the replication of work models, organized as a hierarchy of tasks and exercises. This hierarchy extends from the simple to the complex. The essence of this seminal contribution is the ability to replicate interactions. The learner makes a response to the work-model simulator; the work-model simulator immediately presents feedback as to how the learner's response will affect the system."[16]

Boschmann: "The adjective 'interactive' refers to the capacity of the software and hardware to give the user the opportunity to make

choices and process that input to create an individualized path
through the software. This creates a *personalized learning experience that is useful as a stand-alone learning experience.*"[17]

Nickerson: "Computers can simulate dynamic processes of considerable complexity. And, all with student-directed exploration and ma-
nipulation. Time can be compressed or expanded, allowing a wide
variety of experimentation. Thus, there is the opportunity to create
a new generation of teaching laboratories."[18]

Again, it should be underscored that the value of the interactive
capacity of the computer is that it adapts the learning experience
to the *needs of the individual rather than the availability of the
teacher to provide one-on-one tutoring*. This crucial matter is subsequently explored further.

COMPUTERS AND EDUCATION:
SELF-DIRECTED LEARNING

Another dimension to the unique potential of computers is that—
theoretically—curricula can be designed that, to varying degrees,
progressively allow learners to phase into directing their own learning
experience, particularly at the higher levels. Exploring this matter
further:

In 1972, the Carnegie Commission on Higher Education made this
observation: "The new technology holds two major promises for students. The first is that they will *become more active agents* in their own
education. The second is that they will have more flexibility and variety in their education."[19] Later, in 1988, Gardner sharpened the focus
on this matter of self-directed learning by suggesting that "with age
and experience, curricula should take *an increasingly individual fla-
vor.*"[20]

It can be noted that in kindergarten, the classes are small and the
personalized direction from the teacher is great. In middle and high
schools, the class size begins to increase and more self-direction
is expected from learners. There is an additional progression of this
pattern in college. Finally, in graduate education, the learner be-

comes a scholar with a mentor for consultation and guidance. Self-direction is a requisite and original discovery is a key ingredient of the protocol.

Pertinent in this progression is the learner's capacity to seek and utilize information independently. This also increases at each educational level. The term paper based on prescribed texts in seventh grade progresses to the research thesis in graduate school. Again, the degree of self-directed effort also escalates incrementally.

In the context of this discussion, a pattern emerges regarding the phased introduction of computers and the Internet into the teaching-learning process. Obviously, the initial goal is to have learners attain *computer literacy*. Next, the learner can experience progressively greater increments of self-directed learning by computer. In the early grades, the teacher-directed curriculum prescribes exactly how and when the learner will use the computer. At a later point, the learner becomes proficient in "surfing the Internet" to discover and subsequently utilize new information.

Ideally, all of this occurs in the context of a predetermined curriculum *under the guidance and direction of the teacher*. In discussing the teacher's role, it is necessary to face head-on the pragmatic, sensitive matter of the computer's capability to replace teachers. This is an issue that appears to bring into sharp focus a *critical* philosophical dilemma.

On the one hand, there is the long-standing, deeply ingrained, intuitive belief that teaching and learning is a process *driven by the interaction of two committed humans—the teacher and the learner*. On the other hand is the realization that a mind coupled to a multimedia, interactive information-management system can, without question, learn many things—on an individualized, self-directed basis.

In chapter 7, the Technology-Enhanced Curriculum is introduced. This is a carefully crafted strategy that deals pragmatically with this intricate matter. In this model, teachers *maintain their traditional, critical lead role* in the classroom. However, they will be empowered with customized computer systems designed—as previously noted—to extend and amplify their capacity to provide one-on-one tutoring which is individualized to the specific needs of a particular learner—rather than the availability of the teacher. And all are integrated precisely into the curriculum—*in the traditional manner*.

THE NEW LITERACY AND EDUCATION

This chapter began with the speculation that computers and related technology would propel humankind to a new level of evolution. This is based on the reality that from the beginning of time all major advances in how individuals communicate served as powerful catalysts for progress. Undoubtedly, the personal computer ranks as a major advance, and already its impact has been profound.

To fully appreciate the computer's potential in education, it is necessary to comprehend the concept of what has come to be called the *new literacy*. In the broadest perspective, the time has come to redefine *literacy* in a more generic, contemporary context. Simply, it is "an individual's capacity to store, retrieve, and transmit information."

To take this concept further, it is suggested the term *video literacy* refers to the individual's capacity to store, retrieve, and transmit information through the use of video technology, and it is aligned with the term *computer literacy*. Therefore, it can be reasoned that contemporary society utilizes three literacy modes: *print literacy, video literacy,* and *computer literacy*.

Perception

At the beginning of the twenty-first century, it is apparent that society is driven by information managed in three literacy modes: print literacy, video literacy, and computer literacy. To maximally empower teachers, all three should be integrated into the implementation of the curriculum. What is not apparent is how this is best accomplished.

The term *multimedia* has been in vogue for several decades. It refers to combinations of print, graphics, sounds, and images of all types, still and motion. Although the various media are integrated or linked by virtue of the message, storage and retrieval require the use of multiple systems and devices. Additionally, multimedia is designed to be retrieved in a predetermined sequence and pace.

The computer changes all of this. What it does is now referred to as *convergence:* the storage and retrieval of multimedia by one information system. This is *interactive multimedia*—the compelling power of computers.

Convergence has been described as "the intersection of the richness of movies with *depth* of print with the *interactivity* of computers." Additionally, the incredibly rapid penetration of computers into every aspect of contemporary society translates into a rapidly increasing dependency on interactive multimedia. Thus, the term *convergence* is superseded by a broader, more descriptive term—the *"new literacy."*[21]

Perception

Interactive multimedia, stored and retrieved by computer, represents a linkage, or convergence, of print literacy, video literacy, and computer literacy. Its growing importance in contemporary society suggests it be identified by the term the new literacy. Its full potential in the classroom is significant and still to be realized.

THE NEW LITERACY APPLIED

To fully understand the new literacy and its enormous implications for *amplifying the teacher's capacity to function*, it should be useful to review some fundamental conclusions put forth in earlier chapters:

The teaching-learning process is *driven—or fueled—by information.* Although there is much more to the process, nothing happens unless at some point information is made available to the learner.

The *fidelity* of the information, in great part, determines the effectiveness of the process. When it is necessary to use a replica, as it is most often, the *smaller* the discrepancy between *replica* and *referent*—or the *higher* the fidelity of the information—the *better* the outcome of the process.

Also, in regard to the fidelity, it has been proposed that *a verbal description of anything that can be seen must be considered a compromise.* Specifically, a verbal description alone only stimulates the left brain; a verbal description along with an image stimulates the whole brain.

The relevancy and accessibility of the information to that particular learner—the "individualization" factor—also impacts the outcome of the teaching-learning process.

Perception

The new literacy—interactive multimedia—offers teachers the opportunity to improve the fidelity, the relevancy, and the accessibility of the information driving the teaching-learning process and thus enhance student achievement.

To demonstrate the validity of this conclusion the following real-life learning experience is depicted. It is at the highest educational level and therefore is intended to demonstrate the ultimate utilization of educational technology:

A second-year medical student is learning how to diagnose valvular heart disease in preparation for her clinical rotation. The traditional curriculum at this advanced level of education includes a great deal of self-directed learning; class sessions in which the teacher customarily provides a slide-illustrated lecture; and, most important, at one point, elbow-to-elbow instruction by the clinical teacher in the patient-care setting.

The *traditional approach* to preparing for the clinical experience consists mainly of reviewing lecture notes and reading the textbook: several pages are devoted to the etiology of valvular heart disease. This includes a diagram of a defective valve, a verbal description of where the defect exists, and how it impairs normal cardiac function. To assist in diagnosing the condition, a number of symptoms are described in the text, including the sounds of a defective heart valve. It is noted, for instance, that a normal valve sounds like "flub-dub." A defective valve sounds like "flub-dub-dub." Finally, the clinical procedure for securing the final diagnosis is described by the text. This is followed by a listing of treatment alternatives and their relative effectiveness.

At this point, the learner is considered prepared for hands-on clinical experience.

The *Digital Age* approach to preparing for the clinical experience would include the *new literacy*—by computer: several frames of text are devoted to reviewing the etiology of the condition, which are followed by video sequences showing the development of the defect in the fetal heart. By animation, the consequences of the valvular defect on the circulation of blood are demonstrated.

Then, a segment of tape using fiber-optic video to view the defective heart valve as it actually functions, and the learner also hears the actual heart sounds. These are then compared with the sounds of a normal heart.

A video of someone actually performing each step of the clinical procedure for securing the diagnosis is shown. The learner has control of sequencing and pace. Demonstration of treatment alternatives with data on their relative effectiveness follows the video.

The learner is then given an on-screen examination that includes text, visuals, and sounds. Based on the results, the material not adequately learned is reviewed until a predetermined performance level is achieved.

The computer system provides the learner with a quick-reference printout of the salient points regarding diagnosis and treatment that includes sample prescriptions of the drugs indicated.

The learner is now prepared for the clinical learning experience—*at the elbow of the teacher.*

This is a reality-based example of the use of computer-generated, whole-brain interactive multimedia—the *new literacy*. It clearly represents an improvement in the fidelity, relevance, and accessibility of the information made available to the learner. Further, it demonstrates how teachers can adapt the new literacy to the traditional teaching-learning process—it is an evolutionary approach. Is it *necessary* to do research to determine which of the two approaches is more effective?

COMPUTERS AND EDUCATION: THE STATE OF THE UNION

Where are we now in the day-to-day curriculum-integrated use of computers in the classroom? The most authoritative current source of information is the study by the Office of Technology Assessment of the U.S. Congress that was completed in 1995. It offers the following conclusions (all italics added):

Over the past decade, schools have spent approximately $500 million on new computers alone.
Computers are used relatively *infrequently* for teaching and learning in traditional academic subjects.

The need to closely integrate technology with the curriculum is generally acknowledged. However, the way technology is to be integrated is *less clear*.

By the spring of 1995, U.S. schools will have 3.8 million computers in place—about one for every nine students. Nevertheless, a *substantial* number of teachers still report *little or no use* of computers for instruction.[22]

According to still another report: as is occurring throughout the nation, there are extensive efforts to reform education in the Commonwealth of Kentucky. The law mandating change was passed in 1990 as the Kentucky Education Reform Act (KERA). Among a host of measures, it proposed that over a six-year period, $560 million be spent for networks, hardware, and software. In October 1995, five years into the effort, the report of a study conducted by the University of Kentucky was released. It focused on the implementation of what is called the Kentucky Education Technology System. The summary follows:

A significant effort for development and training will be needed for technology to reach its full potential as a tool for teaching and learning. Word processing received considerable use in the study schools. Spreadsheets and databases are beginning to be a part of regular instruction. However, information technology was rarely observed being used for instruction. [23]

Perception

There is ample evidence that after more than a quarter century of high expectations, dedicated effort, and substantial expenditures, computers have failed to improve what happens in the classroom. Additionally, it appears there has been no serious attempt to analyze and thereby learn from this failure.

LEARNING FROM FAILURE: A PROPOSAL

Chapter 3 offers a detailed analysis of why the full potential of technology in education has not been realized. Now, based on this analysis, an approach to empowering teachers with computers is proposed.

First, however: *killer app* is a commonly used term in Silicon Valley, the capital of the computer industry in the United States. It refers to a major, fundamental breakthrough application of computers in an industry or profession. For instance, in the business world it is the spreadsheet. In air travel it is the scheduling/reservations system. In telephone service it is call routing.

Although many applications of computers in education have been attempted, there is yet to emerge a killer app. This book proposes an application termed *Computerized Remedial Tutoring*, which has the potential of becoming the broad-scaled, basic application of computers in the classroom. It should be generally accepted because—most important—it is uniquely compatible with what traditionally happens in the classroom. Above all, it preserves the teacher's lead role—uncompromised. It is demonstrated in the next chapter.

Perception

The fundamental role of computers in the classroom is to extend the capacity of teachers to provide individualized tutoring to learners, thus compensating for the disparity in each individual's capacity to achieve.

COMPUTERS AND THE NEW LITERACY SUMMARIZED

An understanding of computers, their role in education, and the new literacy is presented in this chapter, based on a series of interrelated basic conclusions derived from this study. To review:

Perception

- As the third millennium begins, it is evident that the development of digital technology has had, and will continue to have, a profound, pervasive impact on the course of global civilization.
- The pervasive societal developments fostered by the computer and the Internet evoke a wide disparity of reactions, since they are perceived from disparate vantage points. Regardless, all can agree on one reality: humans will become more and more dependent on the

mighty, minuscule microchip. We can be optimistic that in the end, the human capacity to adapt will prevail—*as it always has.*

- The computer is a multimedia information-management system that can be programmed to function on an interactive basis. They replicate and markedly amplify certain *basic cognitive functions* of the human mind, specifically storage, computation, and retrieval. Thus, computers have *enormous potential to profoundly impact* the teaching-earning process.

- The mind coupled with a computer infinitely amplifies its capacity to perform the basic cognitive functions. Yet, there is no configuration of microchips that replicates the intricate, vital interface between mind and emotions—*a basic limitation of computers.*

- Computers *actively* engage the human mind and create a synergy. However, nothing transpires unless the human takes the initiative to interact; and then the mind is locked into an active, progressive, collaborative thinking mode. Thus, in a sense, using a computer can be considered *aerobics for the mind.*

- Computer technology has been *adapted* to amplify the capacity of professionals in virtually every aspect of society—with the *exception* of the teacher. Rationalizing this reality becomes increasingly difficult, since teaching and learning is an information-intensive process.

- There is a generalized intuitive feeling that computers should have a vital role in teaching and learning. What is lacking is a sharply focused definition of that role and a strategy for integrating computers into education alongside books and chalkboards—*in a mode that secures the teacher's central role.*

- Because computers store multimedia information interactively retrievable utilizing software that is course-specific, they allow teachers to provide each member of the class an increased number of individualized learning experiences based on the *learner's needs rather than the teacher's availability.*

- At the beginning of the twenty-first century, it is apparent that society is driven by information managed in three literacy modes: *print* literacy, *video* literacy, and *computer* literacy. To maximally empower teachers, all three should be integrated into the implementation of the curriculum. What is not apparent is *how* this is best accomplished.

- Interactive multimedia, stored and retrieved by computer, represents a linkage, or convergence, of print literacy, video literacy, and computer literacy. Its growing importance in contemporary society suggests it be identified by the term the *new literacy*. Its full potential in the classroom is significant and still to be realized.

- The *new literacy*—interactive multimedia—offers teachers the opportunity to improve *the fidelity, the relevancy,* and *the accessibility* of the information driving the teaching-learning process and thus enhance student achievement.

- There is ample evidence that after more than a quarter century of high expectations, dedicated effort, and substantial expenditures, computers have failed to improve what happens in the classroom. Additionally, it appears there has been no serious attempt to analyze and thereby *learn from this failure*.

- The fundamental role of computers in the classroom is to extend the capacity of teachers to provide *individualized* tutoring to learners, thus compensating for the disparity in each individual's capacity to achieve.

ONE FINAL THOUGHT

It can be said that computers and the Internet provide society with a global harvest of ideas and information. Unfortunately, we still haven't found an effective way to have this remarkable harvest fuel the teaching/learning process. When we do, it will undoubtedly have a monumental impact.

NOTES

1. Zey, Michael G., *Seizing the Future: How the Coming Revolution in Science, Technology, and Industry Will Expand the Frontiers of Human Potential and Reshape the Planet*. New York: Simon and Schuster, 1994, p. 216.

2. Ogden, Michael R., "Politics in a Parallel Universe: Is There a Future for Cyberdemocracy?" *Futures*. No. 26, September 1994, p. 713.

3. Koelsch, Frank, *The Infomedia Revolution: How It Is Changing Our World and Your Life*. Toronto, Ontario: McGraw-Hill Ryerson, 1995, p. 108.

4. Floridi, Luciano, "Internet: Which Future for Organized Knowledge, Frankenstein or Pygmalion?" *Information Society*. January/March 1996, p. 5.

5. Stoll, Clifford, *Silicon Snake Oil: Second Thoughts on the Information Highway*. New York: Doubleday, 1995, p. 7.

6. Perelman, Lewis J., *School's Out*. New York: Avon, 1992, p. 51.

7. Perelman, *School's Out*, p. 49.

8. Thornburg, David D., *Education in the Communication Age*. San Carlos, CA: Thornburg and Starsong, 1994, p. 173.

9. Thompson, James J., *Instructional Communication*. New York: American Book Company, 1969, p. 227.

10. Cuban, Larry, *Teachers and Machines*. New York: Teachers College Press, 1986, p. 35.

11. Thompson, *Instructional Communication*, p. 158.

12. Bunderson, Victor C., "The Evolution of Computer-Aided Educational Delivery Systems," in *Instructional Technology: Foundations*, ed. Robert Gagne. Hillsdale, NJ: Lawrence Erlbaum, 1987, p. 283.

13. Halal, William E., "Telelearning: The Multimedia Revolution in Education," *Futurist*. November 1994, p. 21.

14. "Clinton Wants Faster Internet, Computers in Every Classroom." *Lexington Herald-Leader*, October 11, 1996, p. A3.

15. Schwier, Richard A., "Current Issues in Interactive Design," in *Instructional Technology: Past, Present and Future*, ed. Gary Anglin. Englewood, CO: Libraries Unlimited, 1991, p. 195.

16. Bunderson, "Evolution," p. 311.

17. Boschmann, Erwin, *The Electronic Classroom: A Handbook for Education in the Electronic Environment*. Medford, NJ: Learned Information, 1995, p. 71.

18. Nickerson, Raymond S., "The Context of Education," in *Technology in Education: Looking toward 2020*, ed. Raymond S. Nickerson and Phillip Zodhates. Hillsdale, NJ: Lawrence Erlbaum, 1988, p. 286.

19. Carnegie Foundation for the Advancement of Teaching, *The Fourth Revolution: Instructional Technology in Higher Education*. Hightstown, NJ: McGraw-Hill, 1972, p. 75.

20. Gardner, Howard, "Mobilizing Resources for Individual-Centered Education," in *Technology in Education: Looking toward 2020*. Hillsdale, NJ: Lawrence Erlbaum, 1988, p. 106.

21. Tyler, Keith I., *Educational Communication in a Revolutionary Age*. Worthington, OH: Jones, 1973, p. 40; Haney, John B., *Educational Communication and Technology*. Dubuque: Wm. C. Brown, 1980, p. 107.

22 U.S. Congress, Office of Technology Assessment, *Teachers and Technology: Making the Connection*. OTA-EHR-616. Washington, DC: U.S. Government Printing Office, 1995, p. 46.

23. University of Kentucky, The Institute on Education Reform. *The Implementation of the Kentucky Education Technology System*. Frankfort: Kentucky Institute for Education Research, 1995, p. x.

7

TEACHERS EMPOWERED: THE TECHNOLOGY-ENHANCED CURRICULUM

A teacher is the source of caring and reassurance in the midst of a long-term, anxiety-provoking experience.

—Michael T. Romano

About this chapter:

- It describes a new strategy to deal with the old challenge of empowering teachers with technology.
- It lists the criteria used in designing the so-called Technology-Enhanced Curriculum.
- It depicts the proposed new operational model in a real-life classroom situation.
- It defines the features of the proposed new curriculum.
- It identifies some of the issues that need to be addressed in implementing the proposed "adaptation model" of education.

THE ADAPTATION MODEL: A NEW STRATEGY

Two new models of education will be proposed based on the "stages of instructional evolution" suggested by the landmark Apple Classroom of Tomorrow project.[1]

The *adaptation model* is one in which "technology is thoroughly inte-grated into the classroom in support of existing practice." It is an interim stage essential to reaching the *transformation model* where "technology is a catalyst for significant changes in learning practice; where students and teachers adopt new roles and relationships."

Although ACOT specified a rational two-stage process for phasing technology into schools, it stopped short of actually defining a new working model of education. This essential next step is described in the hope that the new strategy will take us beyond the present impasse re-garding how to effectively connect teachers, learners, and technology.

The Technology-Enhanced Curriculum is offered as an entry-level, interim model designed to meet three primary criteria:

- Empower teachers with technology so they can do what they do—better;
- Be maximally compatible with the system in place so it can be im-plemented with maximum ease and minimal disruption; and
- Put in place the enabling measures required to eventually phase in the ultimate Digital Age *transformation* model.

EMPOWERING VIRGINIA ROBERTSON WITH TECHNOLOGY

Time: 8:45 A.M.; first day, new semester; hopefully, the near future.
Place: Central High School, Everytown, USA.

Virginia Robertson has taught ninth-grade American history for 27 years. She likes what she does, and over the years her rewards have been many and meaningful. She has been voted "best teacher of the year" four times in her career.

Now, it is another new semester, and in 15 minutes they will be sitting before her—new faces, new personalities, new minds, and, most impor-tant—new responsibilities. There is always a special pulse palpable throughout the building on the first day. But, this year, for Virginia, the throb is somewhat more pronounced. It is the first time through many reform cycles—she has survived them all—that she feels good about what is going to happen. The reform is called the Technology-Enhanced

Curriculum, and she believes in the changes. This time, the new has been carefully folded into the old; she feels amply prepared and confident. Virginia Robertson is guardedly enthusiastic.

Now, there are only five minutes and, out of habit, she double-checks to make sure the essentials are in place. The chalkboard is beginning-of-the-semester clean. In the trough there are four fresh sticks of chalk, two new board erasers, and her trusty pointer. On her desk: the roll book, the textbook, a stack of handouts, and for the first time ever—a digital video-disc player remote control with her name on it. There is also a DVD labeled "American History, Unit I, Session 1." Next to the disc is a softcover book entitled *American History, Unit I, Session 1: Teacher Syllabus*.

It is nine o'clock and as always, they are straggling in, vibrating with their familiar chatter and laughter. Now, it is time to close the door, stand before the desk with a semiserious demeanor until they are quiet, and, finally—the plunge into the critical first encounter. "I'm Mrs. Virginia Robertson and I teach ninth-grade American history. Are you all in the right room?" . . . pause . . . "Good! Let's start with an understanding— maybe we should call it sort of a commitment: I promise to give you my best, and in return I expect you to give me your best. Do we have a deal?" . . . pause . . . "Good. Let's move on.

"The course is divided into units, corresponding to the chapters in your textbook. Each unit is spread over a two-week period and consists of eight one-hour sessions held in this room. Then, we will have one two-hour session held in the computer laboratory. In the one-hour sessions, I'll be your guide as we explore by video *the sights and sounds of history—as it happened*. You may have heard, this new feature of your curriculum is called Teacher-Narrated Video. I think you're going to find it exciting. As usual, I'll provide ample opportunity for us to discuss what you've seen and heard and what you've read in the textbook assignments.

"So that you can give your full attention to looking and listening and so that your mind is free to question and discuss anything, you will not be burdened by note taking. At the end of each class, you will be given handouts containing the session's highlights. Any questions?" . . . pause . . . "Oh, one more thing: in order to keep developing your writing skills, you will prepare a 10-page term paper using the Internet, plus the library, for your reference material. I know you've already had experience using both, but we will discuss that part of the course later.

"Now, about the two-hour session in the computer lab: I will be there with you, and we will be joined by the school's computer specialist, Dr. Brian Teague. You will begin by taking an on-screen examination. It will be based on the class sessions, the handouts, and the textbook assignments. The examination will include the usual type of questions, plus a new type in which you will be expected to identify and comment on details of the video segments I presented in class. As soon as you finish, there will be a readout of your grade, and, immediately, the computer will go into a tutorial mode based on those parts of the exam you missed. This is called Computerized Remedial Tutoring, and it is programmed to respond specifically to each of your individual needs. Save your questions about this for our first session with Dr. Teague. I know this is a new experience, but I'll be there with him to guide you through it.

"Finally, because of our new Technology-Enhanced Curriculum, the passing grade is now 90 instead of 70. What that really means is that each of you now has the opportunity to *learn more than those who took the course last year*." Mrs. Robertson picks up the DVD, walks over to the DVD/TV console, and inserts the disc. Then, remote in hand, she pauses for a moment, eyeballs the class, and pushes the play button. The guided tour through American history begins.

On the screen there appears what seems to be a front-view close-up of a rather large, wooden desk. There is no title, no music, no sound at all—just a front-view close-up of a large, wooden desk. *The learners look. The learners wonder. The learners' minds are engaged.* . . . A few moments pass, and then a door on the front of the desk opens and out crawls a little, delightfully impish boy about two years old. Still no music, no narration, just the gleeful noises of a playful child. . . . Now, the scene slowly widens as the little boy makes his way to the front of the desk where a man is seated. He embraces him joyfully, and the man places the child on his lap as they begin to chat playfully.

Then, Mrs. Robertson pushes the pause button, and the delightful scene becomes a still picture. She turns to the class, "Who are these people and where are they?" A number of hands are raised eagerly. Since this is the first day of class and she doesn't as yet connect faces with names, she looks down at her open roll book. "Tracy Montgomery, what do you think?" "President John F. Kennedy and John-John in the Oval Office," Tracy answers. "Correct," says Mrs. Robertson. She pushes the stop button, and the screen is blank. Then, she walks to the chalkboard, picks up a piece of chalk, and writes in bold letters, "John Fitzgerald Kennedy."

For the next several minutes, Mrs. Robertson does what she does so well: she interacts with her learners as they go through the highlights of JFK's early life; his heritage, family, marriage, and early political career. All the key facts are written on the board—as always.

Now, back to the remote, and on the magic screen two men appear, each at a podium. For the next two or three minutes, each in turn speaks. There are close-ups of their faces. One appears somewhat ill at ease and very serious; the other projects casual confidence and a special charisma. The serious one has the shadow of a beard, and perspiration is visible on his upper lip. Again the pause button, and the image is frozen.

A glance at the roll book, "Lee Hale, who are these men and what are they doing?" He answers, "That's John Kennedy debating Richard Nixon. It was the first time a presidential debate was televised." "Correct. Very good, Lee. You can read more about the debate in your textbook. But now, let's go over the issues of the 1960 campaign." Again, it's back to the chalkboard, and for the next 20 minutes, the teacher elicits information from the learners and—as always—notes the key facts with chalk.

It is a situation of minds interacting with minds—both sides, right and left! It is a synergism of textbook, chalkboard, electronic images and sounds, and—above all—a skilled teacher empowered with technology. It is the teaching-learning process at a new, evolutionary level. It is powerful. It is engaging. It closes the technology gap between the classroom and the world beyond its walls.

For the next seven sessions, the learners—hand in hand with Mrs. Robertson—become witnesses to history. She is the narrator standing next to the TV monitor as *they see, hear, and feel* the exciting times of the Kennedy presidency. There is the drama of the election returns, the traditional pageantry of the inauguration, the keen disappointment of the Bay of Pigs, the intense anxiety of the Cuban missile crisis, the high exhilaration of the speech at the Berlin Wall, and the heartbreak—the terrible heartbreak—of the assassination; and *all in sight and sound.* They are there. They literally are witnesses. To add texture and depth, they absorb information from the textbook—as always.

But there is more—much more.

In physics, Mr. Wilson begins the year with a four-session overview of the physical phenomena to be covered in the course. Narrating over video segments of the 1969 moon footage, he skillfully guides his class from the colossal launchpad to a tiny spot on the eerie surface of the moon; and all of this from the perspective of the many laws of physics that had to be managed—with infinite care—to make this unprecedented feat possible.

In sociology, Miss Pinto escorts her class to a magnificent spring ball, held on the eve of the Civil War in an elegant Southern mansion. To create the grand illusion, she uses segments of the epic 1939 motion picture *Gone with the Wind*. The music, the refreshments, the finery, the furnishings, even the mores of the day are all authentically depicted as Rhett Butler dances with the newly widowed Scarlett O'Hara. *And Miss Pinto's class is there—eavesdropping, learning.*

In chemistry, Mr. Funk uses video created by computer graphics to carefully construct complex molecules. Then, as if by magic, he combines two, initiating a reaction depicted in slow motion, although it really occurs in a flash: intriguing, multi-element structures disassembling and reassembling in new, intricate configurations, and all orchestrated by a skilled teacher—*empowered with technology.*

Then, there is Mrs. Pelosi who teaches English literature. At the push of a button, she has King Lear leap from the pages of the textbook onto the face of the magic tube. And so, she shares with the class her all-time favorite Shakespearean actor—the incomparable Richard Burton. At selected intervals, he is put on hold *as the teacher and learners talk, read aloud, interact, enjoy—and learn.*

This is the power of the new, mind-grabbing Teacher-Narrated Video. But back to Mrs. Robertson's American history class. They are ready for their first session in the computer lab.

"Good morning, my name is Dr. Brian Teague and I'm here to help you through what I know will be an exciting, valuable, new experience. These computers have been programmed with software specifically created for your course. They will find out what each of you has learned in your first unit of American history and, also, pinpoint what you have not learned. The computers are programmed to tutor each of you so that we can close the gap between what you already know and what Mrs. Robertson thinks you should know to complete unit one with a grade of at least 90. If you don't get your 90 in this two-hour period, you will be provided additional time later.

"Actually, it's as though each of you will have Mrs. Robertson at your elbow to help you better understand the material in unit one. We call it Computerized Remedial Tutoring, and it's all part of our new Technology-Enhanced Curriculum. During this two-hour session, I will be here to help you deal with the computer. Mrs. Robertson will be here to help you with the course material. Now, let's get started."

Virginia Robertson looks on as her class proceeds. She feels good about what is happening. Each of her learners is being provided what she has always strived to deliver: ample, additional, individualized tutoring so he or she might attain a higher level of achievement. Indeed, Mrs. Robertson's own capacity to function has been amplified. And, for the first time in her career, she truly feels empowered—by technology.

A real-life classroom episode has been depicted. It is a classroom in which the traditional teaching-learning process has been enhanced by interposing between teacher and learner the core information technologies—video and computers. A classroom in which the teacher has more capacity to function than ever before possible. A classroom in which the technology gap has been closed—a Digital Age classroom.

A REALITY CHECK

The depiction of the Technology-Enhanced Curriculum is not intended to be about

- whether Teacher-Narrated Video is best delivered to a class by a videocassette, DVD, or CD-ROM;
- whether it is better to substitute a term paper for taking notes in class;
- whether it is feasible to raise the passing grade 20 points, 10 points—or at all;
- whether two hours of Computerized Remedial Tutoring time for each eight hours of classroom time is the optimal mix;
- whether it is best to locate computers in a classroom or in a laboratory; or

- whether every teacher requires the assistance of a computer specialist to provide her learners with Computerized Remedial Tutoring.

In actually implementing the envisioned Technology-Enhanced Curriculum, it is essential that all these matters—and a host of others—be
approached and sorted out. Undoubtedly, how these details are managed will vary from situation to situation and will have an impact on the
final result. However, these variables must be considered tangential to
the crux of what is presently being proposed here.

Additionally, the Technology-Enhanced Curriculum is not proposed as
the leading edge of the vast potential of information technology in education. There are teachers who have advanced beyond Teacher-Narrated
Video and Computerized Remedial Tutoring, but it has been established,
conclusively, that these are the few. The many are still firmly entrenched
behind a host of barriers and still teach as they, their parents, and their
grandparents were taught. In essence, the new strategy brought forth is
about how to at last penetrate these formidable barriers and make the
elusive connection between teachers, learners, and technology.

REVIEWING THE FEATURES OF THE TECHNOLOGY-
ENHANCED CURRICULUM

1. The Technology-Enanced Curriculum (TEC) is optimally compatible with what traditionally happens in classrooms. Most important, the teacher's role remains essentially unchanged.

   - Technology is integrated directly into the routine presentation of
     the curriculum, any curriculum, at any level.
   - The teacher's responsibility for implementing the curriculum re-
     mains intact; no new understandings are required.
   - There is no major modification of the teacher's traditional role; it
     should not be anxiety-provoking.
   - It builds upon a system already proved effective, one that has
     been in place for generations.
   - A major retraining of teachers is not required; it can even be im-
     plemented by those not technically versatile.

2. The TEC amplifies the teacher's capacity to function. It strategically interposes technology at the interface of teacher and learner. Specifically, it empowers teachers allowing them to *plan, communicate, guide,* and *evaluate* more effectively.

   - How teachers and learners interact is enhanced, rather than the system surrounding that critical interaction being merely modified.
   - The essential, traditional bond between teacher and learner remains uncompromised.

3. The TEC utilizes television in a new interactive format. With Teacher-Narrated Video, the teacher's role is amplified rather than preempted. The format adapts video to the traditional routine of the classroom; teachers remain in total control.

   - Teachers remain at the front of the room doing what they do best—presenting information and interacting with learners.
   - The *compromise of only using verbal descriptions of all that can be seen and heard* is eliminated; thus, teachers provide information of greater *fidelity*.
   - A new, visually rich, dynamic experience is created for learners, and it stimulates *both* the right and left sides of the brain.

4. The TEC utilizes the interaction/individualization capacity of computers. With Computerized Remedial Tutoring using course-specific software, the teacher is able to provide learners access to additional assistance targeted specifically to each individual's *needs,* not the *availability* of the teacher.

   - A compelling, personalized, new dimension is added to evaluation: instant feedback followed by remedial tutoring.
   - The inherent disparity in each learner's capacity to learn what is taught in a particular course is addressed directly.
   - Traditional teacher-directed group-learning experiences are supplemented with individualized, self-directed, self-paced learning experiences by computer.

- Course-specific software provides precise integration of the computer experience with the content and scheduling of the curriculum.
- It is proposed as the basic, universally adaptable application of computers in education, an application that can be designed as an integral component of all curricula at any level.
- The many other specialized adaptations of computer technology to education are not precluded.
- Teacher computer literacy is not a requirement, thus eliminating a major barrier to realizing the potential of computers in the classroom.

5. The TEC requires technology that is already in place in most schools. It represents an entry-level, basic technology platform upon which teachers can build.

- The teacher can progress to additional, more sophisticated applications, including use of the Internet.
- It can serve as a template—or a standard—for equipping all schools with hardware; none exists today.
- For the first time, it bases hardware requirements on the specific needs of a curriculum, rather than an arbitrary determination.

6. The TEC represents a natural progression beyond what presently happens in the classroom. It is measured, managed evolution and can be put in place without new, additional research.

- It is based on the rationale that the existing system is not the result of focused, long-term research; rather, it evolved over the centuries. Progressive steps were taken when it was apparent they would work.
- Finally, some of the research and demonstration results of the past 40 years are applied. The computer's effectiveness in providing remedial tutoring has been confirmed over and over again.[2]
- Based on the transition from radio to television in the living room, there should be no hesitation regarding the effectiveness of supplementing teacher-talk with Teacher-Narrated Video in the classroom.

- All parties involved will be able to readily adapt to the measured increment of change, and the new is firmly linked to what is already in place. It is an example of where less is more.

7. The TEC is driven primarily by new, curriculum-integrated, custom-designed, course-specific software. The electronic courseware, coupled with the textbook and interaction orchestrated by the teacher, creates the heightened synergism of whole-brain, interactive multimedia—the *new literacy*—in the classroom.

   - The critical role of course-specific software has been underscored repeatedly in the literature, including sources as authoritative as the Apple Classroom of Tomorrow project[3] and the study conducted by the U.S. Congress.[4]
   - It confirms that the emphasis must be shifted from hardware to software. Until a support matrix is created which allows teachers to use course-specific, curriculum-integrated software, the full potential of technology will not be realized.

These are the features of the Technology-Enhanced Curriculum. It should be noted again that what has been described is a *transitional* model necessary to implement the ultimate Digital Age Technology-Dependent Curriculum.

One final, very critical point: *the Mrs. Robertson depicted is more than a source of information or the manager of a curriculum. She is the source of caring and reassurance to learners in the midst of a long-term, anxiety-provoking experience. She is the source of motivation and guidance. She is a vital role model and the indispensable element of the classroom equation. And, let it be emphasized again: the Technology-Enhanced Curriculum preserves and protects her unique, traditional role.*

THE INTRIGUING MATTER OF THE PASSING GRADE

How long would an automobile manufacturer survive if some of the products it turned out met only 70 percent of its own design standards? How much confidence should you have in a physician who may know only 70 percent of what his or her medical school specified physicians should know?

There is in place an educational system that has traditionally accepted 70 as a passing grade. In reality, this implies that 30 percent of what is taught—any 30 percent—*doesn't have to be learned*. Thus, it must be concluded that the existing teaching-learning process has an output with up to 30 percent disparity in quality. And it appears that traditionally a great deal of effort is expended to help learners cross that mystical passing-grade line but little to find the means to narrow the 30-percent gap.

Outside the classroom, the computer is applied routinely to improving quality and then maintaining standards in processes ranging from making lollipops to producing jet airliners. Under no circumstances would a 30-percent disparity in quality be tolerated.

Computerized Remedial Tutoring coupled with Teacher-Narrated Video offers the intriguing possibility of compensating for the inherent disparity in the learners' aptitude and narrowing the 30-percent quality gap in the output of the teaching-learning process. Admittedly, it is a conjecture—an *intriguing* conjecture.

SOME ISSUES TO BE ADDRESSED

The Technology-Enhanced Curriculum is, in reality, only a concept. Those who would make a commitment to this approach should be prepared to face the challenge of identifying all the many, formidable issues to be addressed—one at a time—if the concept is to become a reality.

In the next chapter, these central matters are explored: *what does implementation entail? approximately what would it cost? and how might it be funded?* There are a host of additional questions that must be addressed if the proposed reform is to be deemed at all feasible. Some of the more obvious include the following:

- How do you deal with the additional time required for Computerized Remedial Tutoring? Extend school hours? Extend the school year?
- Should learners with lower grades receive priority in using computers in situations where availability is limited?

- How do national achievement scores and college entrance requirements deal with learners whose passing grade may have been extended beyond 70 by the Technology-Enhanced Curriculum?
- How do you compensate in grading learners who have computers
  at home? Should they be provided take-home software?
- How are learners best exposed to the Internet without experienc-
  ing information overload and all its negative consequences?
- In new school construction, should computers be housed in a cen-
  tralized facility or in each classroom?

Undoubtedly, the list of questions included here is only a first step toward devising an implementation strategy for the Technology-Enhanced
Curriculum. But at least the critical first step has been taken—a concept
has been conceived. One that hopefully signals the beginning of the end
of decades of tentativeness and groping regarding the role of technology
in the classroom, that ushers in an era of confident utilization, and, at
long last, that *elevates technology in the classroom to a level commensu-
rate with the book and the chalkboard.*

ONE FINAL THOUGHT

The viability of any new approach in education in great part depends
upon the teacher's acceptance. In 1997, after reading an early draft of
this chapter, the president of the Kentucky Education Association (the
teachers' union), Janet Carrico, expressed this opinion: "I am very impressed with this concept. After reading chapter 7, I became very excited about the potential of the Technology-Enhanced Curriculum. I
think you are right on target."[5]

NOTES

1. Sandholtz, J., Ringstaff, C., and Dwyer, D. *Teaching with Technology*. New
York: Teachers College Press, 1997, p. 37.
2. Boschmann, Erwin, *The Electronic Classroom: A Handbook for Education
in the Electronic Environment*. Medford, NJ: Learned Information, 1995, p. 71.

3. Fisher, Charles, Dwyer, David, and Yocam, Keith, *Education and Technology*. San Francisco: Apple Press, 1996, p. 200.

4. U.S. Congress, Office of Technology Assessment, *Teachers and Technology: Making the Connection*. OTA-EHR-616. Washington, DC: U.S. Government Printing Office, 1995, p. 125.

5. Personal written communication between Janet A. Carrico and Michael T. Romano, November 3, 1997.

MAKING IT HAPPEN: A NEW STRATEGY FOR AN OLD CHALLENGE

Some will say that technology and education are doomed as partners for one moves too quickly and the other too slowly.

—Charles Fisher, "Learning to Compute and Computing to Learn"

About this chapter:

- It begins by underscoring the magnitude of the challenge to achieve broad-scaled, quantifiable improvement in learner achievement.
- It describes what is involved in bringing the Technology-Enhanced Curriculum to the classroom.
- It proposes a formula for making a working cost estimate.
- It reviews the controversial matter of standards in education.
- It proposes a range of implementation strategies.

AN OPENING PERSPECTIVE

In 1998, writing in *Education Week,* a retired teacher offered this view:

We should stop all efforts at school reform. No more wasted billions. No more schemes leaving damaged kids in their wake. We know there has

never been any real success in school reform. Therefore, let's resume traditional methods: *a teacher in a classroom with a chalkboard, a piece of
chalk, a textbook and a classroom full of willing students who want to be
there.* [italics added][1]

As a recurrent theme throughout this book, I have contended we can
get beyond frustration and defeatism by analyzing and then dealing effectively with the barriers to long-term, meaningful education reform.
Bacchetti offers this view: "If we are to reform public education, we have
to accept its complexity and have the patience and determination—
indeed, the collective courage—to analyze, understand, and respond to
that complexity. With Albert Einstein, we should seek to 'make things as
simple as possible but not simpler.'"[2]

The proposed Technology-Enhanced Curriculum is a simple concept.
The implementation strategy described in this chapter is also straightforward. However, as Bacchetti notes, *making it happen* inevitably requires patience, determination, and collective courage.

Fisher was insightful when he wrote: "Some will say that technology
and education are doomed as partners for one moves too quickly and
the other too slowly."[3]

MANAGING CHANGE IN EDUCATION: SOME BASIC GUIDELINES

In colleges of business administration throughout the nation's universities, *institutional change* is now considered an academic discipline. As
an administrator in a university health center responsible for new program development, it was necessary that I keep abreast of the literature
in my field. Over the years, it has been possible to derive from a rather
large body of knowledge several universal guidelines that are particularly pertinent to managing change in education:

1. Worthy goals alone do not ensure success; often a sound concept is
   discredited and discarded because of faulty implementation. Thus, it
   is essential that failures be thoroughly and openly analyzed, and,
   where indicated, alternative implementation strategies be attempted.

2. In a free society individuals have the right to criticize and/or reject what has been proposed, and they have the implicit *responsibility* to offer alternatives; this should not be optional. Only then can we generate meaningful constructive discussion and minimize the cacophony of negativism that too often compromises efforts to effect change.

3. Proceed on the premise that the rate of change and the increment of change possible in any given situation are inversely proportional to the number of people involved. Broad-scaled education reform, because of its scope, is a slow, demanding, tedious process; thus, it will take longer to achieve than most people expect. A proficient change manager will maintain momentum without compromising critical elements of the implementation plan.

4. In the initial phase of the change process, we must clearly define goals in terms of the outcomes expected. Also, the consequences of not taking effective action must be specified. An understanding of *why* it has to be done should precede an agreement of *what* has to be done and *how*. Most important, criteria for measuring outcomes should be in place.

5. The new must be deliberately tied to the old with as many "strings" as possible since, for most, displacing the familiar with the unfamiliar is at the least anxiety-provoking. It has been suggested that a sound plan *must respect the past, represent the present, and reflect the future*.[4]

6. Underscore to all parties that, inevitably, all progress exacts a toll. Identify obvious trade-offs at the front end of the process so that there are few surprises—if any. In education reform, teachers and learners must adjust to new, unfamiliar operational patterns. At the least, the toll is temporary disruption.

7. Keeping those involved motivated is a demanding aspect of managing the change process. The line between allowing pressure to be a "stimulant" or an "irritant" is easy to cross. As in the systems of a living organism, irritants are invariably rejected or "walled off." Those attempting to maintain motivation must be skilled in human relations and group dynamics as their role is critical.

SOFTWARE PRODUCTION: WHAT IS INVOLVED

Implementing the Technology-Enhanced Curriculum involves creating a teacher-support system capable of creating custom-designed, curriculum-specific courseware. As previously noted, the challenge is demanding. However, it is similar to what the education establishment accomplished in the 1960s when it tooled-up for live and recorded television productions for the classroom.

It is envisioned that existing curricula would be converted, or retrofitted, with the new course-specific electronic materials. Thus, what to teach and when to teach it would remain unchanged. It would merely involve altering the "how" aspect of the process. Specifically, it involves producing video segments for Teacher-Narrated Video and computer software for Computerized Remedial Tutoring. These would be integrated with the curriculum in place and with each other.

The literature confirms the fact that the classroom teacher has not been trained to play the lead role in video production and computer software development; additionally, the teachers could not make the time commitment.[5] This effort would be accomplished by what might be termed a conversion team, consisting basically of a video producer, a computer programmer, and, to ensure the academic integrity of the material, a master-teacher/subject-matter expert, equal in stature to a textbook author. There is, of course, nothing immutable about this mix; it can be modified according to the circumstances existing at a particular site.

This conversion effort is economically feasible because a wealth of film and video, which can readily be converted to the new formats required for the Technology-Enhanced Curriculum, already exists. The combined libraries of the news networks, Hollywood, the Public Broadcasting System, C-Span, the Arts and Entertainment Network, the Discovery Channel, and the History Channel have it all. Every event in human history, every major literary work, and every natural or physical phenomenon is already "in the can." Access to these materials should not be difficult.

Another enabling factor is the existence of a cadre of media professionals who, for decades, have specialized in producing educational films and television. These individuals are based at universities and educational television networks throughout the country. Undoubtedly, they could be recruited to participate in the process.

Finally, to ensure that the new courseware/software would be maxi-mally curriculum-specific, the conversion team would be provided copies of all print materials, including texts, manuals, handouts, exami-nations, and all course-related audiovisual materials such as films, videos, and slides. As the ultimate enabling measure, the course session to be converted might be videotaped with a fixed, unmanned camera. This would provide a valuable replica of the actual course session to as-sist the team in producing the software.

What has been described represents a beginning toward creating a protocol for implementing a *curriculum conversion process*. One thing is certain: the teachers of specific courses being converted should have the responsibility for final review and approval of the new materials produced.

APPROACHING THE CRITICAL MATTER OF COST

To determine a preliminary working estimate of the cost of producing the video courseware and computer software for Mrs. Virginia Robert-son's ninth-grade American history course, the following assumptions and cost estimates are suggested:

1. The course is scheduled for five sessions per week for 30 weeks, a total of 150 sessions.
2. Each eighth presentation is followed by two sessions at the com-puter.
3. Each presentation includes six minutes of video segments; each two sessions at the computer will require one computer program.
4. The course requires a total of 12 hours of video and 15 computer programs.
5. Each hour of video is estimated to cost $50,000; each computer program, $25,000.

Based on these assumptions, it would cost $975,000 to convert Mrs. Robertson's course. If it is assumed that in a total K–12 program there is an average of five courses per year equivalent to Mrs. Robertson's course, it would cost approximately $44 million to convert nine years of a K–12 program in a school district, assuming each school in the district employs a similar curriculum. *The critical matter of standardization is discussed subsequently.* To keep the $44 million price tag in perspective:

- Considering the enormity of the task, converting an entire K–12 curriculum would require a minimum of five years. Thus, the $44 million cost would be prorated to $8.8 million per year.
- In 2001, the total expenditure for educational technology in the 50 states was budgeted at $5.7 billion.
- In 1995, the U.S. Congress Office of Technology Assessment estimated that in all the Department of Education programs, the educational technology components totaled $8.8 billion.[6] In 2001, the amount budgeted exclusively for technology was $872 million.
- To support one K–12 conversion for each state, the federal government would have to commit $440 million per year for five years.
- Since 1991, the relatively small state of Kentucky spent over $660 million to promote the use of educational technology.

Several references have been made in this book to the 10-year Apple Classroom of Tomorrow project initiated in 1986. It was conceived and implemented by a blue-ribbon group of nationally recognized education theorists and funded by a major computer manufacturer. The goal was to improve learner achievement by providing each learner and each teacher two computers: one for the classroom and one for the home. A comparison between the ACOT approach and the Technology-Enhanced Curriculum (TEC) indicates the following:

- Based on a cost per computer of $750, implementing the ACOT concept nationally for 50 million K–12 learners and 8 million teachers would cost an estimated $87 billion.
- Converting one K–12 curriculum per state to the TEC for the 50 states would cost $22 billion.
- The ACOT conversion provides funds for hardware only; the software requirements are undetermined and not included in the cost.
- The TEC conversion produces software for existing curricula and can utilize hardware already in place.

These preliminary estimates and comparisons lead to the conclusion that, although the cost of putting in place the Technology-Enhanced Curriculum is substantial, *it is certainly not prohibitive for the United States.* It is obvious that initiating such a costly program at the local, state, or national level must be preceded by a credible demonstration project.

One final perspective: consider what it takes to amplify the capacity of a surgeon beyond removing gallbladders to replacing hearts. It was necessary to put in place a complex, costly, team-centered support system. This reality also applies to pilots, bankers, and other professionals. To markedly improve learner achievement, the same must be done to empower teachers. There simply is no other way.

THE STANDARDIZATION DEBATE

Standardizing curricula is a key factor in considering the feasibility of implementing the Technology-Enhanced Curriculum. The investment in course-specific software depends upon the number of different curricula to be converted. It is relevant that in 1999, writing in *Education Week,* Hoff said, "The expense of digital content has joined the issue of standardization."[7]

The term *standardization* in education translates into *controversy.* Over the past several decades, this particular debate has ebbed and flowed many times. The ramifications include no less than the classroom teacher's basic prerogatives, the role of administration, the book publishers' lobby, the interface with the political system, the power of the teachers' unions, and a host of other "heavy" issues. In the last decade of the twentieth century, a great deal of progress was made in standardizing curricula at the state level—more than most people expected.

Let it be understood that it will be possible to implement the Technology-Enhanced Curriculum without bringing closure to the long-standing standardization debate. However, any degree of standardization achieved—at the local, state, or national level—will progressively improve the economic feasibility of putting the proposed reform in place. Thus, a review of the matter is in order in regard to making it happen.

Basically, the term *standardization* refers to setting achievement standards, centralizing the evaluation process, and utilizing a standard curriculum. *The three are inevitably linked.* It is common for politicians and others to talk of national achievement standards without "dropping the other two shoes."

Achievement standards within a district, a state, or the nation can only be evaluated by centrally administered examinations; and the results are not comparable unless there is in place a uniform, standardized curriculum. Comparison with others is not important to those scoring well. However, those whose scores are at the low end understandably fall back on the position that the schools "do not teach to the test." Thus, in the final analysis, standardized achievement scores are only comparable and meaningful when standardized curricula are in place. *This truth cannot be evaded.*

The standardization debate, at varying degrees of intensity, has been a part of the educational landscape for decades. In 1995, the president of the National Council for Accreditation of Teacher Education aptly expressed the views of the proponents of the status quo:

> Rather than merely "covering the curriculum," teachers are expected to connect with the needs of all learners and to prepare all students for thinking work—for framing problems, finding and integrating information, creating new solutions, learning on their own and working cooperatively. *Such teaching cannot be produced through teacher-proof materials or regulated curricula.* (italics added)[8]

On the other hand, in 1972, an eminent group of educators assembled by the Carnegie Foundation issued a widely applauded report urging the extensive use of technology in education. It was called *The Fourth Revolution,* and it made a compelling case for standardizing and sharing high-cost software.[9] That was more than a quarter of a century ago. Yet, this matter with far-reaching implications is still being debated.

What has been reported in the literature is as follows:

- Diane Ravitch, a former assistant secretary of education, did an extensive study of standards in U.S. education. In her book published in 1995, she concluded that Americans expect standards in many aspects of their lives: building codes, standards to protect food and drinking water, health and safety standards in restaurants and factories, maintenance and security standards for airlines, and so forth. Thus, she believes it follows that they should expect standards in the classroom.[10]

- Kantrowitz and Wingert, writing on schools worldwide, concluded that consistency is the key to the excellence observed overseas. Most industrialized countries have a national curriculum. Routinely, teachers get specific instructions. Our educational system has always reflected the American credo of independence. The authors note, "Everyone does their own thing to the point where a fifth-grade teacher can't count on a fourth-grade teacher having taught certain things."[11]

- Perelman, an outspoken critic of the American education establishment, noted that schools and teachers test their own students, evaluate their own performance, and certify their results with self-issued diplomas. Measurement processes affect every aspect of our national education and training systems. Measurement problems thwart attempts at innovation and reform.[12]

Understandably, teachers have a legitimate vested interest in the standardization debate. What is at stake here are their traditional prerogatives in determining what happens once the classroom door is closed. Their views are generally reflected in the position taken by their unions. Thus, it is pertinent to report on the views expressed by Albert Shanker, the long-time president of the American Federation of Teachers until his death in 1997. In 1991, he wrote:

- If anyone had talked about a common curriculum for U.S. schools a few years ago, people would have said he was crazy. Sure, that's the way they do it in most other industrialized countries; and, sure, their students achieve at a much higher level than ours. But the education systems in those countries are under the control of their central governments, and the idea of our federal government dictating what children learn in local schools was out of the question. *Now, we have begun to understand the price we pay for our fragmented curriculum.*

- A common curriculum means that there is agreement about what students ought to know and be able to do and, often, about the age or grade at which they should be able to accomplish these goals. In the U.S. we have no such agreement about curriculum—and *there is little connection between what students are supposed to learn, the knowledge on which they are assessed, and what we expect our teachers to know.*

- Another disadvantage of not having a common curriculum is that we don't have any agreement on what teachers need to know. Colleges and universities can't train teachers on the basis of the curriculum they are going to teach or assess them on how well they know it. (italics added)[13]

Later, in 1995, Shanker commented on the proposal by the federal government to create national achievement standards:

- Almost every industrial nation requires students to take subject-matter examinations created at the regional or national level, but many American educators strongly oppose the idea. *"You can't fatten up cattle by weighing them.* You have to feed them," is a typical U.S. response.
- What's wrong with the American way of doing it? When students are assessed relative to their fellow students (using measures like grades and class rank) rather than relative to an absolute standard, students have a personal interest in *persuading each other not to study*.
- Also, when there are no external standards, teachers are under pressure to *lower their own standards* so that more students look as though they're doing well. In New York State, 58 percent of the teacher leaders responded "Yes" to the question, "Is there pressure on your teachers to pass students who don't earn a passing grade?" Under a system of external norms, teachers and administration can't do this.
- External national or regional exams make a big difference. *Weighing the cattle may not make them fatter, but the cattle are more likely to be well fed if the seller knows that the buyer is going to weigh them.* (italics added)[14]

These views, expressed by the leadership of a major teachers' union, are extremely significant. Undoubtedly, they reflect a degree of change from the teacher's traditional position in the debate on standards. This in turn has also had an impact on the national political leadership. In 1996, both the president and vice president of the United States went on record vigorously supporting national achievement standards. As a political strategy, they would not take this bold position unless they believed that the unions' views would not be an insurmountable hurdle. Again, it should be noted that national achievement standards mean externally administered examinations; and that, inevitably, all of this will lead to the realization that a standardized national curriculum is the rational next step.

One final note: columnist David Broder, in a 1997 article, quoted Bob Chase, president of the National Education Association, as saying in blunt language that *"too often NEA has sat on the sidelines of change, naysaying, quick to say what won't work and slow to say what will. The fact is that, in some instances, we have used our power to block uncomfortable changes, to protect the narrow interest of our members, and not to advance the interests of students and schools."* Broder concluded that this statement signaled a revolutionary break from tradition for Chase's group, which counts 2.5 million teachers as members. (italics added)[15]

The relevance of the standardization debate to the cost of implementing the Technology-Enhanced Curriculum is obvious. Possibly, recent developments justify guarded optimism. It is as though the stage were set for the convergence of two mighty forces—*technologization* and *standardization,* forces that will have a major impact on how our teachers teach and how our youth learn in the twenty-first century.

ADDITIONAL FACTORS PERTINENT TO IMPLEMENTATION

Before discussing specific implementation strategies, there are four related factors that must be approached:

1. *Higher education and K–12 are different.* The concept of the Technology-Enhanced Curriculum can be considered a *template* applicable to all educational levels. The implementation strategies offered are not. Brock concluded that there can be no single

formula for change common to all of the nation's 3,400 colleges and universities.[16] Thus, the strategies to be discussed here pertain solely to public K–12 education.

2. *Demonstration projects have not had an impact.* Since the educational television demonstration projects of the mid-1950s, literally hundreds of projects have been conducted, costing untold millions and spanning a period of five decades. These efforts were based on the seemingly logical premise that if an innovation could be proved effective at one site, others would eagerly reach out to adopt it. The sites became known as "boutique schools"[17] and "blue ribbon schools."[18] Unfortunately, the broad-scaled adoption hoped for simply did not materialize. The only conclusion to be drawn is that the results obtained were not impressive enough to engender sufficient motivation for change and/or adopting the innovation was simply too complex and demanding.

3. *A catch-22 seems to exist.* The recent U.S. Congress Office of Technology Assessment's extensive survey[19] and the Apple Classroom of Tomorrow's 10-year project[20] have been cited repeatedly in this book. Both are considered authoritative, and both underscore what appears to be a generally accepted mind-set creating a very real dilemma. It has been stated repeatedly that infusing curricula with technology requires an extremely demanding effort. Teachers must play the lead role and assume the major responsibility for the trial and error, the research, and the development required. Unfortunately, it is acknowledged that they have neither the training, the expertise, nor the time to do this. Hence, *the virtual stalemate* and the technology gap in the classroom endure. Catch-22, indeed! The concept and implementation strategy proposed here are intended to bypass this dilemma.

4. *The federal government's role is essential but must be demarcated.* As noted, the cost of implementing the Technology-Enhanced Curriculum is indeed substantial—but not prohibitive if done with federal subsidization. Maintaining local prerogatives while interfacing with the federal government is a long-standing, ongoing balancing act that is performed daily by education and many other segments of society, including health care and aviation.

There are no guarantees; however, when the stakes are high, *the risk must be taken*.

The challenge in approaching implementation was to design strategies that deal realistically with these four critical factors.

A RANGE OF IMPLEMENTATION STRATEGIES

The strategies outlined here are intended as a starting point for discussion. Expectedly, they will raise many difficult questions that must be confronted.

Strategy 1: At the National Level

1. Fund the initiative through the U.S. Department of Education and, to ensure credibility, implement it under the auspices of a national education-related group of suitable stature, perhaps one of the major philanthropic organizations.
2. Create a national advisory committee with broad representation: government at various levels, teachers' unions, and education advocacy groups. They would be charged with developing protocol, assembling the conversion team, selecting the demonstration site, and overseeing the long-term implementation process.
3. Identify the school district in the nation with the highest SAT scores. Recruit it as the demonstration site.
4. Convert that district's entire K–12 curriculum and put in place an evaluation mechanism.
5. Supplement the software package with a video and manual designed to orient classroom teachers to the rationale and implementation of the Technology-Enhanced Curriculum.
6. If the results of the demonstration are positive, offer the complete software package—at the nominal cost of duplication—to any school district in the country, with *no stipulations* regarding how it would be used.
7. Determine on a school-by-school basis what would be required to supplement existing hardware to meet the implementation of the new curriculum.

To elaborate on the protocol of strategy 1:

- Considering the dynamics of the education enterprise, it should be acknowledged at the outset that implementing strategy 1 represents a major challenge and is somewhat idealistic.
- The proposal to convert the existing curriculum of the school district with the highest SAT scores is based on two realities: first, experience indicates that the task of creating a new, nationally accepted curriculum is exceedingly difficult. Second, using the SAT scores to determine the K–12 curriculum that will serve as the standard is a practical way of selecting a program that should have a high degree of acceptability. Undoubtedly, *a number of valid questions* will be raised regarding this approach. Making the software package available at the cost of duplication is in reality making schools "an offer they can't refuse." However, the program is on an entirely voluntary basis, thus safeguarding local prerogatives. Yet, it is anticipated that legislators, parents, and others will expect a compelling explanation from those who choose not to go along with the program.
- Theoretically, this approach may provide the motivation and the impetus for creating a national curriculum without years of demanding, frustrating effort.
- Prior to commencing production of the software, a video and manual must be produced that describe the program. They would be widely distributed so that classroom teachers could be oriented to the Technology-Enhanced Curriculum even before the software is available.
- The hardware requirements for the Technology-Enhanced Curriculum are specific: a TV monitor and a VCR or DVD player placed in each classroom, a teaching laboratory, and, as a beginning, enough computers to provide learners access to the Computerized Remedial Tutoring specified for each course. Because the hardware complement currently existing in schools varies, a mechanism would be devised to determine needs on a case-by-case basis.
- Finally, as previously noted, although the $44 million cost estimate of converting one school district is substantial, it is certainly not prohibitive. In terms of the multibillion-dollar U.S. Department of Education budget, it is reasonable to assume federal funding is entirely

feasible. Strategy 1 represents the lowest cost and the greatest degree of difficulty to implement because it is based on a nationally accepted K–12 curriculum. *The hurdles to be addressed are immense* as it places the issue of a standardized national curriculum in sharp focus. Undoubtedly, this will engender anxiety and controversy.

Strategy 2: At the State Level

This alternative would bypass the difficult issue of a national K–12 curriculum. It proposes that the matter of standardizing curricula be settled on a state-by-state basis. In the past four or five years, great progress has been made to standardize curricula at a state level. The protocol of strategy 2 is essentially the same as strategy 1. However, the federal government would provide a block grant to each state, which would allow it to convert *one* K–12 curriculum. It would be a major interim step toward national standards and would cost 50 times more than strategy 1. The working estimate is $2.2 billion (50 times $44 million). This strategy potentially reduces the number of different curricula from 15,000—the number of school districts in the United States—to only 50, *an accomplishment of major proportions.*

Strategy 3: At the School-District Level

This would essentially leave the present, fragmented system of education in place. The federal government would provide a specific number of matching grants to individual school districts. How many would receive them is to be determined. What combinations of local/federal funds would be required and on what basis the grants would be provided must be sorted out. One thing is certain: this approach would limit the host of derived benefits of putting in place a standardized curriculum, either at the district, state, or national level.

Strategy 4: At the Individual Teacher Level

This would represent a minimal commitment to the proposed concept and, axiomatically, a maximum commitment to the status quo regarding standardization. The federal government would provide matching grants

to individual teachers for the conversion of individual courses, the extent
of the program to be determined on a case by case basis.

ISSUES TO BE RESOLVED

What has been brought forth clearly indicates that the degree of commitment to the proposed reform translates directly into the degree of
commitment to the question of national standards. There is now a future with well-defined options. Clearly, the attempt to implement the
Technology-Enhanced Curriculum translates into this reality: *the drive
for broad-scaled, quantifiable education reform, and national standards
would be joined.*

Further, there has been proposed a range of implementation options
that runs from the bold to the patently timid. These strategies also evoke
issues ranging from the mundane to the profound. Nonetheless, they all
must be approached if the implementation of a workable Technology-
Enhanced Curriculum is to be attempted. Here are some of the more
challenging issues:

- How would the software industry react to having software produced under a federal- or state-sponsored program? Could it possibly be included in the process?
- If federal funds were deployed for the costly curriculum conversion
  process, would it compromise support for existing federal education programs?
- Should the federal government support creating a Technology-
  Enhanced Curriculum and continue to support the many existing
  technology-related programs?
- What would be the posture of the teachers' unions when faced with
  a federal initiative encouraging curriculum standardization?
- Would the demonstration school district selected on the basis of
  SAT scores have any right of ownership to the curriculum-specific
  software created as part of the federal initiative?
- Should the curriculum-specific software produced with federal
  funds be made available to private schools at the nominal cost of
  duplication?

To use a cliché, these questions are only the tip of a huge, menacing ice-
berg capable of sinking even a well-conceived, well-supported education reform effort.

ONE FINAL THOUGHT

There remains one truth: even with a clear vision before us, the ultimate
challenge to achieve broad-scaled, meaningful, lasting, quantifiable improvement in learner achievement in the United States will require a
major effort mounted by a *mighty coalition* of all the legitimate vested
interests. Arms must be linked, conflicting vested interests must be reconciled, and obstacles must be surmounted—at all costs. Perhaps these
expectations are idealistic; perhaps they are not.

Sergiovanni, a professor of education and a senior fellow at the Center for Educational Leadership at Trinity College, makes this admonishment: *"The stakes are high. Finding the right change strategy promises
victory in the national and even international brain race."*[21]

NOTES

1. Kelcher, Evan, "If It Wasn't Around in the Middle Ages It's a Fad," *Education Week*. June 17, 1998, p. 47.

2. Bacchetti, Raymond F., "Staying Power," *Education Week*. November 10,
1999, p. 48.

3. Fisher, Charles, "Learning to Compute and Computing to Learn," in *Education and Technology,* ed. Charles Fisher, David Dwyer, and Keith Yocum.
San Francisco: Apple Press, 1996, p. 126.

4. Romano, Michael T., "Guidelines for a New Department of Operative
Dentistry," *Journal of Dental Education*. Vol. 26, September 1962, p. 247.

5. Darling-Hammond, Linda, Wise, Arthur, and Klein, Stephen, *License to
Teach: Building a Profession for 21st-Century Schools.* Boulder, CO: West-
view, 1995; Thornburg, David, *Education in the Communication Age.* San Carlos, CA: Thornburg and Starsong, 1995, p. 127; Gilbert, Steven, "Making the
Most of a Slow Revolution," *Change*. March/April 1996, p. 23; U.S. Congress,
Office of Technology Assessment, *Teachers and Technology: Making the Connection.* OTA-EHR-616. Washington, DC: U.S. Government Printing Office,
1995, pp. 205, 1, 129, 18.

6. U.S. Congress, OTA, *Teachers and Technology*, p. 96.

7. Hoff, David, "Digital Content and the Curriculum," *Education Week*. September 23, 1999, p. 51.

8. Darling-Hammond, Wise, and Klein, *License to Teach,* p. 96.

9. Carnegie Foundation for the Advancement of Teaching, *The Fourth Revolution: Instructional Technology in Higher Education*. Hightstown, NJ: McGraw-Hill, 1972, p. 84.

10. Ravitch, Diane, *National Standards in American Education: A Citizen's Guide*. Washington, DC: Brookings Institute, 1995, p. 40.

11. Kantrowitz, Barbara and Wingert, Pat, "The Best Schools in the World," *Newsweek*. December 2, 1991.

12. Perelman, Lewis, *School's Out*. New York: Avon, 1992, p. 299.

13. Shanker, Albert, "Developing a Common Curriculum," *New York Times*. February 24, 1991, p. E7.

14. Shanker, Albert, "Feeding and Weighing," *New York Times*. April 9, 1995, p. E6.

15. Broder, David, "Not Enough Meat on the Bone," *Lexington (Ky.) Herald-Leader*. February 17, 1997, p. 24.

16. Brock, William, *An American Imperative: Higher Expectations for Higher Education*. Racine, WI: Johnson Foundation, 1993, p. 64.

17. Cuban, Larry and Tyade, David, *Tinkering toward Utopia: A Century of Public School Reform*. Cambridge, MA: Harvard Press, 1995, p. 120.

18. Riley, Richard, *Best Ideas from America's Blue Ribbon Schools*. Thousand Oaks, CA: Corwin/Sage, 1995, p. 120.

19. U.S. Congress, OTA, *Teachers and Technology*, p. 46.

20. Fisher, Dwyer, and Yocam, *Education and Technology*, p. 20.

21. Sergiovanni, Thomas J., "Changing Educational Change," *Education Week*. February 16, 2000, p. 27.

9

THE ULTIMATE GOAL: THE TECHNOLOGY-DEPENDENT CURRICULUM

The teaching-learning process is driven by the interaction of two committed humans.

—Michael T. Romano

About this chapter:

- It describes a Digital Age "transformation" model of education— the *Technology-Dependent Curriculum*.
- It introduces the concept of putting in place enabling measures before implementing a new, markedly different model.
- It defines the objectives of such a model, thus underscoring the full potential of technology to enhance the teaching-learning process.
- It provides a historical context for understanding the lack of progress in realizing this potential.
- It describes a *learner-support team* and the new role of the master teacher.
- It speculates on a day in the life of a master teacher in the Digital Age.

WHAT SHOULD ENDURE AND WHAT SHOULD NOT

This conviction was derived from more than 40 years as a teacher and a scholar of the teaching-learning process: education is driven by the interaction of two committed humans—the teacher and the learner. It is based on emulation, shared aspirations, and the human need to impact the well-being of others. The relationship between learner and teacher represents a special bond between someone with a "felt" need to grow and someone committed to meeting that need.

Regardless of what we do in education, this *must* endure. On the other hand, there is a mind-set that I believe *should not* endure: the concern harbored by many teachers that technology compromises their role in the educational enterprise. And the hesitation of some to accept the truth that other professionals have grown in stature because their capacity to function has been amplified by technology. An example: the surgeon who removed gallbladders in the 1940s is now transplanting hearts—because of technology.

The Technology-Dependent Curriculum offers the vision of a future in which the teacher continues as one of the most influential individuals in society, and, above all, the learner benefits from a teaching-learning process enhanced by technology.

REFOCUSING ON THE ACOT STUDY

Chapter 1 refers to the "two stages of instructional evolution" based on research from the landmark Apple Classroom of Tomorrow project. Stage 2, termed *transformation,* is the final phase in which "technology is a catalyst for significant changes in learning practice; students and teachers adopt new roles and relationships."[1]

The proposed digital model of education deploys the full power of the technology available today to restructure—*or transform*—the existing model of education. It is not operational without the use of technology.

Again, to review what was noted in chapter 1: the Technology-Dependent Curriculum represents an increment of change beyond anything the existing system could tolerate in one leap. Before it can be implemented, it is essential that an interim model be in place—the

Technology-Enhanced Curriculum—along with a number of additional enabling measures.

THE ENABLING MEASURES

There are prerequisites for mounting all major endeavors. Five are considered essential for creating an operational Digital Age model of education:

- All learners must be competent in traditional literacy and computer literacy no later than the seventh grade.
- When qualified, all learners must have full-time access to their own laptop computer.
- A teacher-support system must be in place to produce and keep updated curriculum-specific courseware.
- Teachers at all levels must be computer literate and versatile in negotiating the Internet.
- Teacher education must prepare them for the new skills required to assume the lead responsibility in the new model, as they did in the old.

The matter of laptops warrants additional comment. After more than 20 years of placing computers in schools, a number of barriers to their efficient utilization have surfaced. One is whether to situate desktop computers in a central location or in the classroom. Regardless of where they are located, the space they occupy is considerable. Further, it is reported that, when in a central location, the chore of scheduling access to desktop computers is demanding, which makes their integration into an ongoing curriculum difficult.[2] Thus, if these barriers are to be eliminated, desktops must eventually be replaced with laptops.

Additionally, the time is rapidly approaching when in middle-class America the rite of passage from childhood to youth will include not only a car but a laptop computer. This next-generation portable creation will exist as virtually an electronic human appendage. It will merge radio, television, CD/DVD player, telephone, and computer. Humans will develop a dependency on a par with having "wheels" parked close by.

Finally, all of this must be considered in terms of a time frame. There are indications the tempo of change in education will accelerate. Still, considering the scope of what needs to happen, even an optimistic view would suggest that it would require at least a decade to put the two models in place—first the Technology-Enhanced Curriculum and then the Technology-Dependent Curriculum.

A TECHNOLOGY-DEPENDENT MODEL OF EDUCATION

The traditional teaching-learning process plays out in variations of three basic settings: the lecture, the teaching laboratory, and the seminar. These would endure in a modified version. How the teacher would function in each of these is transformed by the utilization of technology.

The Lecture

The term *curriculum lock* refers to learners becoming part of a class and progressing through a curriculum at the same pace. It should be noted that seminars and laboratories can be conducted with learners at different points in a course. It is the lecture that requires that all learners in a class be in a lockstep mode *regardless of their aptitude*. Technology allows us to eliminate this major deficiency in the teaching-learning process.

In the Technology-Dependent Curriculum, a series of course modules delivered by computer replace the lecture. The software would be custom produced for that specific course and would

- allow the learner to ask questions at any point to clarify what is being presented;
- provide the heightened sensory perception of multimedia so that what needs to be seen is seen, what needs to be heard is heard, and what needs to be analyzed by graphics is analyzed; and
- include an examination at the end of each module that provides instant feedback and, when necessary, shifts into a tutorial mode based on the learners' identified deficiencies.

The lecture is, for the most part, a passive experience, particularly in higher education where the classes tend to be large. After years of conditioning, the learner sits with mind in low gear, listens, and takes notes. On the other hand, the computer experience described provides one-on-one interaction and thus actively engages the learner's mind. Further, it provides instant feedback on achievement, which serves as a motivational factor.

Most important, when laptop computers are used, learners can retrieve modules *when they want them, where they want them, and as many times as they need them.* Thus, the computer experiences become learner-specific, addressing the disparity in individual aptitudes.

Finally, it can be speculated that by eliminating the chore of lecturing and giving examinations, the teacher is free to assume a more demanding role in managing the educational process, to provide more one-on-one tutoring and guidance. More on this key aspect of the Technology-Dependent Curriculum later.

The Teaching Laboratory

There are two basic varieties of the teaching laboratory. One is intended to demonstrate phenomena and thereby add to comprehension; the other is to teach skills.

In both, the effectiveness of the experience in great part depends upon the learner's understanding of what is to be done and why it is being done prior to actually doing it. A computerized examination would be taken to identify possible deficiencies and provide remedial tutoring. Only after a predetermined level of comprehension is attained can the learner advance to the hands-on phase. It is speculated this will minimize the amount of wasteful trial and error usually associated with teaching labs.

Additionally, the laboratory procedure to be performed is recorded and available on a screen integrated into the workstation. By using a foot control, leaving both hands free to work, the learner views each step in the procedure as many times as necessary immediately before doing it.

An integral design feature of teaching laboratories is a demonstration table equipped with a video image-magnification system. The use of this technology permits teachers to perform scheduled and extemporaneous demonstrations, thus providing reinforcement to learners as they attempt to master the procedure. Although this application of video technology has been reported in the literature for more than 40 years, most existing teaching laboratories do not include this useful technological accoutrement.

Further, when the objective is to learn a skill, a camcorder can be used to record the learner's performance. Then, an elbow-to-elbow critique is provided by the teacher, resulting in a meaningful, personalized experience for the learner.

Finally, the range of phenomena to be studied and skills to be mastered can be expanded markedly by computer-generated virtual reality simulation techniques. Thus, the limitations of size, complexity, and cost of experiments can be eliminated, allowing a new generation of laboratory experiences.

The Seminar

The seminar is an age-old, teacher-managed mode that has new prominence in the envisioned Digital Age model of education. It is here that minds can interact with minds, *creating a synergism that drives the teaching-learning process to new, heightened levels.*

The envisioned design of this high-tech facility incorporates state-of-the-art image-presentation technology. The focal point is a large rear-projection screen. It displays multimedia information originating from a variety of video and computer sources. Linkage is to the Internet, an intranet, and video networks. This technology should be available in all group-presentation facilities from seminar rooms to auditoriums.

The new-generation *technoseminar* format is loosely structured to allow exploration and interaction involving learners, teachers, and other participants recorded or electronically brought in live from any location. These extramural participants can be scheduled or presented extemporaneously depending on how the discussion unfolds. Additionally, the Internet and intranet serve as an information reservoir to be tapped when required.

The effectiveness of this potentially engrossing learning experience depends upon the skill of the individual who orchestrates it—the Digital Age master teacher. This highly skilled person must be a subject-matter expert, who is adept at fostering interaction and capable of utilizing sophisticated technology. Undoubtedly, this evolutionary, demanding role for teachers will require appropriate modifications in teacher training.

A point to be underscored: in the Digital Age model of education, the passivity of the lecture is replaced with the mind-grabbing interaction of the *technoseminar*. Additionally, this enhanced format provides the heightened sensory perception of multimedia.

Finally, the technoseminar format can be designed to accommodate learners within a range of perhaps four course modules. This mix of learners at varying levels will foster a degree of interaction that should add a powerful new dimension to an age-old format. *The effectiveness depends on a skilled teacher empowered with Digital Age technology.*

HUMAN RESOURCES REQUIREMENTS

The implementation of the technology-dependent model of education requires a new, expanded complement of personnel. It happened in health care, in air travel, and in most other segments of our technological society. It is a pattern where roles become progressively differentiated, resulting in the evolution of teams. For example, compare the operating-room team required to transplant a heart with the team required to remove an appendix.

It is envisioned that the teacher's capacity to function needs to be extended through the use of auxiliary personnel. Again, medical education serves as the model. The master teacher functions with *a learner-support team*—just as does the attending physician in a hospital. The master teacher's team includes those working toward their degrees at both the undergraduate and graduate levels. The primary role of this cadre of teachers-in-training is to assist the master teacher in providing learners day-to-day guidance/counseling and one-on-one instruction.

When a learner experiences difficulty beyond the auxiliary's capacity to help, the individual is referred to the master teacher. If necessary, a still higher level of expertise is available—the school district's cadre of behavioral counselors.

The teachers-in-training also function in a variety of one-on-one laboratory teaching assignments. As these individuals advance, they are provided experience in conducting technoseminars—the most demanding assignment.

Following is a summary of the new, evolutionary role of the master teacher. He or she

- serves as the primary subject-matter expert; understands how to access the myriad reservoirs of information on the Internet; keeps abreast of new subject-matter developments; in higher education, is involved in research;
- functions as the head or coach of the *learner-support team;* assumes primary responsibility for the learner's progress; guides the development of the teachers-in-training;
- counsels learners when they have difficulties beyond the capabilities of the auxiliaries; decides when to refer learners to the school district's behavioral counselors;
- assumes responsibility for monitoring the achievement of learners; also, evaluates teachers-in-training;
- understands how to use information technology based on utilization strategies devised by specialists; is capable of detecting malfunctions in hardware and software and when to refer problems to the in-house technology staff; and
- has the ability to conduct the new generation of technoseminars; orchestrates the interaction of learners, teachers, extramural participants, and technology; and is critical to the effectiveness of this primary learning experience.

Producing manpower for the Digital Age model of education requires modifications of teacher-training programs. The curricula must be altered to prepare the newly defined master teacher. Additionally, the present extramural student teacher and teacher intern programs must be redefined.

This will require sorting out a number of intricate issues. One is coping with the marked disparity in the quality of the host schools for the teachers-in-training. Does the answer involve expanding the number of traditional teacher-college-model laboratory schools? Or defining and adhering to stricter criteria for host schools? Optimistically, when the goals are clear and the challenges well defined, the chance that obstacles will be surmounted increases.

A final matter: in the past, schools and colleges have developed the capacity to provide learners meals and transportation. Now, an additional in-house capability must be developed: technology-support services. These services are available in academic medical centers where technology is an integral part of teaching and patient care. This need is based on the reality that teachers do not have the expertise to design technological systems, produce the curriculum-specific courseware, and then ensure its reliability.

DEFINING THE OBJECTIVES

The Technology-Dependent Curriculum is designed to achieve five primary objectives:

1. *Provide learners more individualized attention.* The concept of the three-tiered *learner-support team* described earlier evolved from the drive in the last half of the twentieth century to create smaller classes. The axiom is elemental: smaller classes permit more individualized attention, resulting in better learning.

   Funding is the major factor limiting lower teacher-learner ratios. Expanding and restructuring college of education student teacher/intern programs provides a source of low-cost human resources for schools. It should be noted again that this tried-and-true system has been in place for more than a century in medical education. Expectedly, adapting it to teacher education will raise a number of issues that must be resolved.

   The value of increasing one-on-one interaction between teacher and learner cannot be questioned. The challenge has been to find the means.

2. *Provide learners the opportunity to progress at an individualized pace.* Unquestionably, there is a disparity in learners' aptitudes. For the most part, this translates into a disparity in the time required to meet achievement standards. Traditionally, youth are sorted by age, placed in classes, and required to progress in lockstep. To compensate for the disparity in aptitudes, an arbitrary passing grade, usually 70, was established. In essence, this implies that 30 percent—any 30 percent—of what is taught does not have to be learned. The possibility that technology would

eliminate this apparent compromise has been considered for decades.

In 1967, I shared my views on where the union of education and technology was leading. In an article published in the *Annals of the New York Academy of Sciences,* I posed this question regarding education in the 1990s: "Would we want our academic programs to be readily adaptable to the varying aptitudes of learners so that they would reach similar goals at their own pace?"[3]

The merits of individually paced learning appear as obvious today as they were in 1967. Over the intervening decades, many have attempted implementation. Today, there is still no generally accepted model suitable for all levels of education.

The Technology-Dependent Curriculum utilizes the computer to break the traditional lockstep mode required by the lecture. The course material is available to the learner on an individualized basis rather than a group basis and includes instant evaluation and remedial tutoring. Most important, *learners have the choice of time, place, and pace.*

It is essential that the model include mechanisms to control the extent of the individualized pacing. Some learners will require that the pacing be closely supervised. At the other end of the aptitude spectrum, other learners will be capable of progressing with a minimum amount of teacher oversight. All of this is possible because there is in place a computerized monitoring system continuously providing the teacher with information regarding the learners' progress based on the readout from individually dedicated computers.

The value of individually paced education has been acknowledged for decades. The challenge has been to find the means.

3. *Create a more compelling, whole-brain learning experience by fueling the teaching-learning process with interactive multimedia.* The concept of information being the fuel that drives the teaching-learning process is discussed fully in chapter 4. If this analogy is rational, it follows that the nature of that fuel has a direct bearing on the outcome of the process.

A computer-generated graphic of a human heart pumping blood, illustrating the function of each structure, plus the heart sounds is obviously more effective than a diagram in a textbook with a four-page verbal description. Allowing learners to retrieve this digital graphic from a laptop computer when they want it, where they want it, and *as many times as they need it* is also an obvious advantage.

How does this computer-generated graphic retrieved from a laptop compare with sitting in a class of 50, looking at a static diagram of a heart projected on a screen, with the teacher providing a verbal description of how it works while the learner takes notes?

There can be no doubt that a motion picture with sound, available on an individualized basis is more compelling than a still picture with a verbal description. More than pictures and graphics in motion, computerized multimedia add the powerful dimension of interactivity, a feature that customizes the experience to the aptitude of the individual learner.

Finally, there is the concept of multimedia and the right/left brain phenomenon noted in chapter 2. In her book *Teaching for the Two-Sided Mind*, Williams writes:

> The brain has two hemispheres but too often the education system operates as though there were only one. Students are expected to learn most of their information from books and lectures. They work almost exclusively with words and numbers, in a world of images, symbols and abstractions. It is important to recognize that computers offer exciting possibilities for stimulating right hemisphere learning.[4]

Her work and that of others support the contention that computer-generated, interactive multimedia provides a heightened, whole-brain sensory experience for learners. The value seems obvious; the challenge, again, has been to find the means.

4. *Allow the mind to develop a broader range of capacities—a higher evolutionary level.* In 1967, after more than 10 years of work in applying technology to the teaching-learning process, I shared this view:

> It is with great anticipation that we await the emancipation of the human mind from the yoke of memorization. Computers and the simplification of information storage and retrieval by other technology

will make virtually any information available any time, anywhere through a pocket-sized device that will emerge as a vital new appendage to the human body. Who can tell what new powers the mind will develop?[5]

Now it is the twenty-first century, and wearing a laptop by shoulder strap is the new Digital Age status symbol, and the next generation of miniaturized, pocket-sized marvels is already on the scene. Kurzweil, writing in *The Futurist*, believes that within the next decade people will have at least a dozen computers on and around their bodies, each dedicated to a specialized information monitoring/retrieval function.[6]

For now, let us speculate on the impact of computers on young, developing minds as an outcome of the envisioned Digital Age model of education. Not only will the mind be freed of much of the chore of storing and retrieving facts, it will be conditioned by a powerful impetus—interactivity.

Computers lock the mind into a pattern of responses. Nothing happens unless the mind interacts with the machine. In a sense, computers provide what can be termed "aerobics for the mind"— a potentially potent stimulus. Thornburg notes: "Interactivity is rewarding at many levels. It facilitates creativity and the development of advanced thinking skills."[7]

Therefore, it can be speculated, the proposed model of education would stimulate the mind to advanced levels of deduction, investigation, problem solving, information synthesis, and possibly a higher capacity for self-discipline.

5. *Provide experience in self-directed education for those with suitable aptitudes*. This is an old concept; perhaps its time has come. In 1972, the Carnegie Commission on Higher Education observed: "The new technology holds two major promises for students. The first is that they will become *more active agents in their own education*. The second is that they will have more flexibility and variety in their education" (italics added).[8] This is another expectation yet to be realized. In 1999, two educators wrote: "Students need to be fully and personally engaged in the struggle to learn."[9]

What is self-directed education? It is requiring learners to access, synthesize, and apply the information necessary to realize set course objectives. Essentially, it takes the traditional graduate education experience and moves it to the lower levels. Yet, it is not anticipated that learners could assume this responsibility before high school—if at all.

Why is self-directed education a goal worth pursuing? As the tempo of societal change increases, knowledge and skills become obsolete at an increasingly rapid pace. At the beginning of the twenty-first century the axiom is "What you earn depends upon what you learn." The need for a "lifetime of learning" has been noted since the early 1960s.[10] Naisbitt warns: "People who do not educate themselves—and keep reeducating themselves—will be the *peasants of the information society*."[11]

Digital technology facilitates individual access to vastly expanded reservoirs of information beyond books—specifically, the Internet and computer software. This makes it feasible to include self-directed experiences as part of formal training.

Self-directed education is not for everyone, however. It will evolve as a separate track for those with suitable aptitudes. Eventually, it is possible that entire schools may be dedicated to this approach, for those that qualify.

These are the objectives set for the Technology-Dependent Curriculum. It is the *transformation* model suggested by the Apple Classroom of Tomorrow study. Technology has been adapted to markedly restructure—*transform*—the vital interaction between teacher and learner. It is education for the Digital Age, and, most important, teachers continue to play a central role—*teachers empowered with technology*.

JAMES ROBERTSON, MASTER TEACHER: HIS TYPICAL DAY

Time: 8:45 A.M.; first day, second semester; second decade, twenty-first century.
Place: Central High School; Everytown, USA.

James Robertson has been a master teacher of history for only one semester. He was certified in July after six years at the College of Education, University of Kentucky, and two years as a teacher/intern in Lon-
don, England. After only one semester, he is certain he made the right
career choice. But it was a "no-brainer." His mother, Virginia Robertson,
spent 35 meaningful years in the classroom also teaching history.

Now, as is his routine every morning, he is going over his schedule for
the day to make sure he is prepared.

9 to 10 A.M.
Weekly history department meeting
Agenda:

1. Selection of person to serve on the state History Curriculum
   Council
2. Report from the Committee on the Technoseminar Facility
   Renovation
3. Report from the Committee to Rewrite Student Teacher/
   Intern Manual
4. Review of the current learner achievement data by course of-
   ferings

10 A.M. to noon
Weekly Learner-Support Team Conference
Agenda:

1. Review file of each learner not meeting achievement standards
2. Report on new courseware recently put in use
3. Discussion on counseling/guidance techniques including "challenging encounter of the week"

1 to 3 P.M.
**Serve as moderator for biweekly, four-school ninth-grade American
history technoseminar (four schools participate via intranet).**
Program:

1. Welcome by the host school (rotates among four schools)
2. Learners' re-creation of the 1960 Kennedy–Nixon debate
3. Discussion of the 1960 campaign issues

4. Poll to determine which learner won the debate
5. Live feed from Moscow, Russia; discussion of secret 1960 KGB/Lee Harvey Oswald files, newly discovered by University of Moscow graduate student (contact made on Internet by Central High School history teacher)
6. Discussion regarding impact on the Soviet–U.S. cold war if the secret material had surfaced earlier
7. Summary by a ninth-grader of the technoseminar

3 to 4 P.M.
Consultation with twelfth-grader regarding her participation in an international Internet competition on the production of a curriculum computer module entitled "The Collapse of the Soviet Empire."

Closing his schedule book, Jim Robertson feels comfortable that he is amply prepared to deal with the day's activities. Walking to his 9 A.M. meeting, he has a fleeting thought of the night many years ago when his mother talked at the dinner table about the new Technology-Enhanced Curriculum they were about to implement. "You should see us now, Mom," he thinks, as he enters the conference room and sits down. *The hint of a smile animates his countenance.*

ONE FINAL THOUGHT

The superpowers of the twenty-first century may not be those countries with "super" military might derived from "super" natural resources. Instead, the superpowers will be those countries that find better ways to cultivate the earth's most valuable natural resource, *the incredible human mind.*

NOTES

1. Sandholtz, J., Ringstaff, C., and Dwyer, D., *Teaching with Technology*. New York: Teachers College Press, 1997, p. 37.
2. Fatemi, Eric, ed., "Building the Digital Curriculum," in *Technology Counts '99,* supplement to *Education Week*. September 23, 1999, p. 7.

3. Romano, Michael T., "Health Science Education in the Space Age," *Annals of the New York Academy of Sciences*. Vol. 142, March 1967, p. 349.

4. Williams, Linda V. *Teaching for the Two-Sided Mind*. New York: Simon and Schuster, 1986, p. 7.

5. Romano, "Health Science Education," p. 348.

6. Kurzweil, Ray, "Spiritual Machines: The Merging of Man and Machines," *Futurist*. Vol. 33, November 1999, p. 16.

7. Thornburg, David D., *Education in the Communication Age*. San Carlos, CA: Thornburg and Starsong, 1994, p. 173.

8. Carnegie Foundation for the Advancement of Teaching, *The Fourth Revolution: Instructional Technology in Higher Education*. Hightstown, NJ: McGraw-Hill, 1972, p. 75.

9. Banner, James M. and Cannon, Harold C., "A Student's Best Lesson," *Education Week*. Vol. 19, October 20, 1999, p. 60.

10. Dryer, Bernard V., "Lifetime Learning for Physicians," *Journal of Medical Education*. Vol. 180, 1962, p. 676.

11. John Naisbitt, quoted in Gentry, Cass G., "Educational Technology in the 1990s," in *Instructional Technology: Past, Present, and Future*, ed. Gary Anglin. Englewood, CO: Libraries Unlimited, 1991, p. 27.

⑩

THE WAKE-UP CALL

At a point, public education let go of the old and reached out for the new.

—Michael T. Romano

Admittedly, what follows is a best-case scenario. It is based on the expectation that a number of developments on the educational landscape for some time will inevitably converge. When this happens, the impact will be significant. Education will lift itself into the twenty-first century where it belongs. As a lifelong teacher and an avowed optimist, I am not programmed to speculate in any other way.

Now it is 2020, and the turmoil in education has subsided.

Finally, after a run of more than 150 years, the print-based Industrial Age model of education has been transformed into a technology-based Digital Age model. How did it happen?

The impetus for the transformation was provided by the mighty motivator—*competition*. When, at a point, it came down to maintaining its eminence, the public education establishment in the United States did what had to be done. It let go of the old and reached out for the new. Here are the events that lead to the *"edutech" era of U.S. public education*.

In the first decade of the twenty-first century, the school-voucher movement gained momentum. People had a choice of where to educate their young. To the chagrin of many, funding for public education was increasingly undermined, while the private and for-profit schools began to grow and thrive.

Then, one of the for-profit schools, unfettered by an allegiance to the traditional books, chalkboard, and teacher-talk classroom, made a breakthrough: it implemented a *technology-based curriculum* driven by curriculum-specific courseware. Its report of a dramatic, unprecedented rise in learner achievement scores drew worldwide attention.

In the tradition of American entrepreneurship, the for-profit schools took the next step: they standardized school facilities, curricula, courseware, and hardware. They were then capable of achieving significant economies of scale by readily replicating complete "packaged" schools anywhere. And they continued to grow and thrive.

Then, the inevitable next step: just as had been done in the fast-food, automobile, motion picture, television, and airline industries—packaged schools made their entry into the global marketplace. And the demand far exceeded expectations.

The wake-up call sounded for public education in the United States when one of the for-profit corporations signed a multibillion-dollar, long-term contract with the People's Republic of China to revamp its education system. America's most powerful global competitor was poised to surpass us as a superpower. And with the stakes high and the goals clear, the United States did what it does best: it rose to meet the challenge.

Hence, by 2020, the long-awaited union of technology and public education in the United States became a reality. Youth were being prepared for the demanding Digital Age by teachers whose capacity to function was amplified markedly by technology. And, most important, the traditional, critical, lead role of teachers remained uncompromised. Inevitably, the American public came to the realization that even public education was not immune to the force that makes the United States work so well: *the remarkable power of the free enterprise system.*

INDEX

ABOUT THE AUTHOR

Michael T. Romano has earned international recognition as an educator, administrator, academic health planner, author, and academic software producer. In a career spanning more than four decades, he has served as a consultant in education to the World Health Organization, the U.S. Peace Corps, the National Science Foundation, the U.S. Public Health Service, the U.S. Office of Education, several commercial firms, and a number of academic institutions at home and abroad.

He has held leadership positions in national organizations including president of the Health Education Media Association; chairman of the Council on Medical Television; chairman of the Group on Institutional Planning of the Association of American Medical Colleges; and program chairman of the Kentucky chapter of the World Future Society.

Dr. Romano is currently a professor emeritus at the University of Kentucky and has held faculty and administrative appointments at the University of Pennsylvania, the University of Kentucky, and Louisiana State University. He has the distinction of being a founder of two new dental schools, one at the University of Kentucky and one at Louisiana State University. In 1969, Dr. Romano was appointed president and program director of Health Information Systems, a New York–based company involved in the use of electronic media for the continuing education of health professionals.

He has lectured extensively in the United States, Canada, Europe, and South America. Dr. Romano's contributions to the international literature include 42 articles, chapters in four textbooks, and one coauthored book on the use of television in the health sciences. In addition, he has produced over a hundred educational audiotapes, more than 300 instructional videotapes, approximately a thousand live, closed-circuit instructional telecasts, and two motion pictures.

Presently, Dr. Romano serves as the special assistant to the superintendent of the Williamsburg, Kentucky Independent School District. He provides the leadership for implementing a Technology-Enhanced Curriculum there.